Effective Pupil Grouping in the Primary School

A Practical Guide

Susan Hallam,
Judith Ireson
& Jane Davies

David Fulton Publishers

David Fulton Publishers Ltd
The Chiswick Centre, 414 Chiswick High Road, London W4 5TF

www.fultonpublishers.co.uk

Copyright © Susan Hallam, Judith Ireson and Jane Davies 2002

British Library Cataloguing in Publication Data
A catalogue record for this book is available from the British Library.

ISBN 1–85346–849–5

Typeset by Keyset Composition, Colchester, Essex
Printed and bound in Great Britain by The Cromwell Press Ltd, Trowbridge, Wilts

Contents

Preface

The purpose of this book is to assist teachers and managers within primary schools in making decisions about the types of pupil grouping that they might adopt and to optimise the functioning of those practices within the everyday operation of the school. It is based on research, in particular the findings of two projects. The first, funded by the Institute of Education, University of London, surveyed 2,000 primary schools to establish their current pupil grouping practices and whether they had made any changes recently and, if so, why. The second, funded by the ESRC, involved in-depth case studies of six schools adopting contrasting grouping practices including streaming, setting, cross-age setting, within-class ability groupings and mixed-ability within-class groupings.

In Chapter 1, the historical context of ability grouping is considered and a review of the literature on the effects of ability grouping in the primary school is presented. Chapter 2 explores the current grouping practices adopted in UK primary schools and how schools arrive at decisions about the type of grouping practices to adopt. Chapter 3 describes pupils' experiences when different types of grouping are adopted in the primary school. Chapter 4 explores the strengths and weaknesses of streaming and setting and the impact on pedagogy and the delivery of the curriculum when such practices are adopted. Chapter 5 explores issues relating to within-class grouping, and how different kinds of groupings can be adopted to satisfy different educational outcomes: academic, personal and social. Chapter 6 considers the management of different types of grouping, in particular the allocation of pupils to groups, monitoring of progress and movement between groups. The final chapter explores how schools can adopt evidence-based grouping practices that are sufficiently flexible to meet pupil needs and ensure the best possible educational outcomes: academic, personal and social, for all their pupils.

Acknowledgement

The authors would like to thank all the schools who took part in the research.

Chapter 1

Ability grouping in primary schools

Ability grouping practices in primary schools: the historical context

There is a long tradition of ability grouping in primary schools in the UK. The practice of allocating pupils to classes based on ability (streaming) was widespread in larger primary schools throughout the 1940s and 1950s as pupils were prepared for selection at age 11. During the 1960s, with the move towards comprehensive education, the demise of the 11-plus examination, and an increasing emphasis on equal opportunities, streaming began to decline, further encouraged by the Plowden Report (1967), which advocated a more child-centred approach to primary education. This trend was supported by research indicating that ability grouping had no significant effect on overall attainment, and had negative personal and social consequences for pupils in the lower streams (Jackson 1964; Barker Lunn 1970, 1984). By the 1970s, of those schools that were large enough to stream, only about 20 per cent chose to do so (Bealing 1972; DES 1978). By the 1990s this had declined further to less than 3 per cent (Lee & Croll 1995). Streaming had almost disappeared.

Following the Education Reform Act (1988), the 1990s saw the implementation of the National Curriculum and an emphasis on raising standards. Ability grouping in the form of setting (pupils ability grouped across classes for particular subjects) was perceived as a way to raise attainment and all primary schools were encouraged to introduce it (DfE 1993). This was reinforced by the White Paper *Excellence in schools*, which suggested that setting could be beneficial in raising standards and that 'setting should be the norm in secondary schools. In some cases, it is worth considering in primary schools' (DfEE 1997: 38). More recently, secondary schools have been exhorted to consider express sets, fast-tracking, early entry to GCSE and advanced qualifications for gifted and talented pupils (DfEE 2001a, 2001b). The impact of the DfEE guidance on grouping practices in the primary school will be considered in Chapter 2.

How should we judge the effectiveness of different types of ability grouping?

Whether alternative forms of grouping are seen as effective or not depends on how we define effectiveness and what criteria we use to measure it. Traditionally, primary education in England has had broad educational aims relating to children's academic, personal and social development. Teachers endorse the following five aims. All children should:

- develop their full potential;
- be happy and well balanced;
- have their interest in learning aroused;
- develop self-confidence; and
- be kind and considerate.

(Pollard *et al.* 1994: 109)

Although the Education Reform Act established a statutory obligation on teachers to meet the academic objectives set out in the National Curriculum, teachers did not abandon their non-academic aims. They simply increased their list of objectives. The aims outlined above are broadly in line with those stated in the most recent version of the National Curriculum. This sets out the values and purposes underpinning education in the UK as follows:

> Education influences and reflects the values of society, and the kind of society we want to be. It is important, therefore, to recognise a broad set of common values and purposes that underpin the school curriculum and the work of schools. Foremost is a belief in education, at home and at school, as a route to the spiritual, moral, social, cultural, physical and mental development, and thus the wellbeing, of the individual. Education is also a route to equality of opportunity for all, a healthy and just democracy, a productive economy, and sustainable development. Education should reflect the enduring values that contribute to these ends. These include valuing ourselves, our families and other relationships, the wider groups to which we belong, the diversity in our society and the

environment in which we live. Education should also re-affirm our commitment to the virtues of truth, justice, honesty, trust and a sense of duty.

At the same time, education must enable us to respond positively to the opportunities and challenges of the rapidly changing world in which we live and work. In particular, we need to be prepared to engage as individuals, parents, workers and citizens with economic, social and cultural change, including the continued globalisation of the economy and society, with new work and leisure patterns and with the rapid expansion of communication technologies.

(DfEE/QCA 1999: 10)

From this, two very specific aims are set out:

- to provide opportunities for all pupils to learn and achieve; and
- to promote pupils' spiritual, moral, social and cultural development and prepare all pupils for the opportunities, responsibilities and experiences of life.

These broad aims, encompassing academic, personal and social educational outcomes for pupils, provide a clear framework against which we may assess the effectiveness of different types of ability grouping in the UK.

Types of grouping in primary schools

Primary schools use a range of structured grouping practices and teachers group pupils within the classroom in a variety of ways. Table 1.1 provides a list of the main types of ability grouping used in schools.

Streaming is the most rigid form of ability grouping. Pupils are placed into a class on the basis of a measure of their overall ability and remain in that class for most subjects. It is based on the assumption that individuals have a certain level of general intelligence, which predicts their performance across all subjects and can be measured by objective tests. Banding is a broader form of streaming, which offers greater flexibility as each band contains several classes, providing scope for regrouping within a band. Setting can occur within bands.

Mixed-ability classes are those where pupils are randomly placed in classes which may then be grouped in other ways, for instance through

Table 1.1 Types of ability grouping

Streaming (*tracking*)	Pupils are placed in classes on the basis of a test of their general ability. They remain in their streamed class for most subjects.
Banding	Pupils are placed in two, three or four bands on the basis of a test of their general ability. Each band contains a number of classes and pupils may be regrouped within the band for some subjects.
Mixed ability (*heterogeneous grouping*)	There is no attempt to group together pupils of similar ability or attainment.
Setting (*regrouping*)	Pupils are grouped according to their attainment in a particular subject. Setting may be imposed across a whole year group, across timetable halves, within a band or across mixed-age classes.
Within-class grouping	Pupils are grouped within the class on the basis of ability or in mixed-ability groups. They may be regrouped within the class for different subjects.
Cross-age or vertical grouping (*Cross-grade grouping*)	Pupils in two or more year groups are placed in the same class, for all or part of the curriculum. They may be regrouped by setting or within-class grouping or taught as a mixed-ability class.

setting or within-class grouping. This is the most common form of class allocation in primary schools in the UK. Setting offers a more flexible way of grouping pupils on the basis of their attainment in particular curriculum subjects. Schools may use setting for some or all academic subjects and setting may be introduced in different years. As with streaming, the aim of setting is to enable teachers to match their teaching to pupils' needs. Within-class grouping is the most common form of grouping in primary schools. Groups may be formed on the basis of ability, attainment in particular subjects, friendships or working relationships.

In cross-age grouping, pupils in different year groups are taught together, for all or part of the day. Mixed-age or vertically grouped classes are often necessary in small schools, where there are insufficient numbers to form whole classes each year. Mixed-age classes may also be used for teaching specific parts of the curriculum, with children from several years working together.

What can research tell us about the effects of ability grouping on pupils?

Ability grouping has been the subject of research since the early twentieth century. Since then hundreds of studies have been undertaken and there have been many literature reviews and syntheses of research findings (for recent UK reviews see Sukhnandan & Lee 1998; Ireson & Hallam 1999; Hallam 2002). Much of this effort has attempted to establish whether ability grouping enhances pupils' academic attainment. Researchers have also examined whether ability grouping has any effect on non-academic outcomes, such as pupils' self-esteem, motivation, alienation and attitudes towards school.

Methodological issues in research on ability grouping

When undertaking research on ability grouping researchers face a number of difficulties. First, as indicated above, pupils can be grouped by ability in many different ways, through selective schooling, streaming, banding, setting or within the classroom. Often different types of grouping are in place for children of different ages within the same school. For example, in a primary school, pupils may be in mixed-ability classes for the whole day during Key Stage 1, yet in sets for certain subjects in Key Stage 2. Even when pupils are in mixed-ability classes, individual teachers may group by ability in their classroom for all or part of the curriculum. This makes it difficult for researchers to obtain accurate information about the exact nature and extent of ability grouping within a school and to make comparisons between the effects of each.

Second, a wide range of outcome measures have been adopted to assess effectiveness. These have related to academic, social and personal development. Few projects have taken account of all of them. In addition, researchers use different measures for similar outcomes, making it difficult to compare results from different studies. Academic outcomes have been assessed by performance on commercially standardised tests (especially in reading and mathematics), national tests (e.g. key stage tests), examination performance and course completion. Personal and social outcomes have been assessed using different measures of self-esteem, motivation, attitudes and alienation, or by employing interview techniques. Drawing conclusions across studies is therefore problematic. Generally, a narrow range of learning outcomes has been researched (often reading and mathematics) with little concern for critical thinking, level of understanding, creativity and metacognitive and transferable skills.

A third difficulty is that even within a single school the academic and affective outcomes of grouping are not consistent in size, over time, in different curriculum subjects or with different teachers (Ireson & Hallam 2001). Schools and classrooms are dynamic environments, with many factors affecting learning outcomes. There are complex interactions between grouping strategies, teaching methods, teacher attitudes, curriculum subject, the pacing of lessons and the ethos of the school (Ireson & Hallam 2001). The grouping of pupils is only one of several factors affecting the learning environment of the classroom. The quality of instruction and the curriculum may both mediate the effects of pupil grouping (Creemers 1994). Teachers themselves – through the way they interact with pupils – can be crucial in mediating the effects of grouping (Barker Lunn 1970). These contextual issues have largely been ignored, in particular those relating to the way that grouping is embedded in the ethos of a school and the wider school community. Each school is unique and has its own characteristics relating to its location, pupil intake, size, resources and most importantly the quality of its staff (Mortimore et al. 1988). For this reason, the effects of the same system of pupil grouping may not be consistent between schools, nor even within the same school, as the system is implemented differently by individual teachers.

A final problem is that the effects of grouping are not consistent across groups of pupils. There may be differences relating to ability, ethnicity, age, gender, socio-economic background and other factors. The issue is therefore not whether ability grouping is effective, but for whom and in what ways it is effective and whether anyone suffers as a result of it (Slavin 1987).

School effectiveness research

The evidence from school effectiveness research has demonstrated that there are differences between schools in the extent to which they are successful in promoting the academic and non-academic aspects of children's development. While some schools are effective in promoting academic, social and personal development in children, others are effective only in relation to academic or social and personal development. There is not necessarily a strong association between the effects of school on attainment and other outcomes for pupils. The two dimensions can be largely independent of each other (Mortimore *et al.* 1988).

In a review of the literature on school effectiveness commissioned by Ofsted, 11 factors were identified as key characteristics of effective schools (Sammons *et al.* 1995). Pupil grouping was not included, although there are potential links between most of the factors identified and grouping. Shared aims and goals, which contribute to defining the ethos of a school, are particularly important. How these are related to ability grouping will be considered in Chapter 2. Other key factors included the learning environment, concentration on teaching and learning, purposeful teaching, high expectations, positive reinforcement and monitoring progress, pupil rights and responsibilities and home–school partnerships, all of which may impinge on or be affected by ability grouping.

What are the effects of ability grouping on attainment?

Much of the research on ability grouping has been undertaken to establish whether it is effective in raising pupils' achievement. Researchers have investigated whether average levels of attainment are higher with different types of grouping and the impact on the attainment of particular groups of pupils.

Streaming

When streaming was common practice in UK primary schools, a number of studies were undertaken to explore its effectiveness. Daniels (1961a) found a higher average level of attainment in schools that did not adopt streaming. This appeared to be caused by an increase in attainment of the lower-attaining pupils, rather than the higher-attaining pupils being held back. Blandford (1958), in a comparison of streamed and non-streamed schools, found similar results with a greater spread of scores in streamed schools. Douglas (1964) compared pupils' progress and found that children in the lower streams made much less progress relative to the top streams. The largest study compared pupils in 36 streamed and 36 non-streamed primary schools on a wide range of criteria (Barker Lunn 1970). As many teachers in non-streamed schools practised within-class ability grouping, children in these classes were categorised as being 'streamed'. The findings showed no difference in the average academic performance of boys and girls of comparable ability and social class in streamed or non-streamed schools. Being taught by a teacher who was pro- or anti-streaming also had no effect on achievement, although creativity was higher when pupils were taught by teachers who were opposed to streaming. This appeared to be related to classroom climate, which was more permissive than in the streamed classes. A follow-up study, two years later, showed no difference in performance at secondary school in relation to prior streaming in primary school (Ferri 1971). Similar findings were reported by Daniels (1961b), who compared achievement in streamed and unstreamed schools over a four-year period. He concluded that lower-ability pupils made better progress in unstreamed schools. Gregory (1984), in a review of this early research, described the evidence as mixed but reported that help with reading, targeted at specific ability levels, could improve achievement (Gregory et al. 1982). International reviews of research on streaming in primary schools (Slavin 1987; Kulik & Kulik 1987, 1992; Kulik 1991) have also indicated that streaming has little impact on pupil attainment.

Setting

International reviews of setting (Kulik 1991; Kulik & Kulik 1992) have shown no consistent effects on attainment. Some studies have shown small positive effects, others small negative effects. Overall, the differences have been negligible. When the effects on pupils of high, middle and low-ability have been explored, ability grouping has tended to have a positive impact on higher-ability pupils and a negligible effect on middle- and low-ability groups. A recent UK study explored the effects of setting in the primary school on the progress of over 1,000 pupils in a single local education authority. When the same teaching materials were used for Key Stage 2 mathematics, the test results of pupils in mixed-ability classes were significantly better than those taught in sets. Lower-attaining pupils made better progress in mixed-ability classes, without hindering the progress of higher-attaining pupils (Whitburn 2001).

Vertical or cross-age grouping

Vertical grouping is adopted of necessity when the intake of pupils to a school cannot be allocated to single-year group classes. In some cases, it is adopted because of the perceived educational benefits arising from the social and family-like structure of classes where pupils are taught together by the same teacher for several years (Veenman 1995).

Reviews of pupil attainment have shown no significant differences between vertical grouping and single-age grouping in terms of pupils' academic achievement or social and personal development.

Pupils may also be grouped across grades or year groups in more flexible ways. Cross-age setting occurs when children of similar ability are drawn from more than one year group for particular activities. Reviews of the effects of this, particularly in relation to reading, have been very positive (Slavin 1987; Kulik & Kulik 1992).

Within-class grouping

The most frequently adopted grouping practice in UK primary schools is within-class (see Chapter 2). Teachers group pupils in a variety of ways. Some teachers seat pupils in ability groups for most of the time while others utilise mixed-ability or friendship groups, regrouping pupils by attainment for certain parts of the curriculum or for particular activities (Ireson 1996). Within-class grouping has been shown to be effective in raising attainment, especially in the later years of primary school and when class sizes are large (Lou *et al.* 1996). The effects are greatest in mathematics and science. Pupils of low ability learn more in mixed-ability groups, whereas pupils of average ability learn more in groups of similar ability. High-ability pupils are unaffected by the type of grouping. Both mixed-ability and ability groups produced good results in mathematics and science, whereas ability groupings were better for reading. Working in groups seems to support learning in mathematics and science regardless of the type of group (Kulik & Kulik 1987; Kulik 1991; Slavin 1987).

Enrichment and acceleration

In the USA special classes, acceleration or enrichment classes, are often provided for pupils identified as gifted and talented. The remaining pupils in the school may be in mixed-ability or ability grouped classes. Accelerated classes provide instruction that allows pupils to proceed more rapidly through their schooling or to finish schooling at an earlier age, e.g. compressing the curriculum from four years into three, or extending the calendar to speed up progress by using summer sessions. When compared with children of similar age, accelerated children perform better, but when compared with older children in the age group with which they have been learning, their performance is often worse (Kulik & Kulik 1992; Kulik 1991). In enrichment programmes pupils receive more varied and in-depth educational experiences. Such classes are usually characterised by a challenging education programme with distinctive methods and materials. Reviews of evaluations of such programmes have shown significant gains for talented students in most cases (Kulik 1991; Kulik & Kulik 1992).

Summary

Ability grouping of itself has no clear impact on attainment. Some of the evidence supports ability grouping and some does not. In addition, there are no clear effects for different groups of pupils. The effects on low-, middle- and high-attaining pupils are not consistent. The effects of ability grouping on attainment would appear to be mediated by other factors, including the quality of the teaching and the nature of the curriculum. These will be considered in more depth in Chapters 4 and 5.

Social and personal outcomes of different kinds of grouping

Historically, in the UK, structured ability grouping was found to have negative effects on the personal and social development of pupils. In this section we consider what we know about the effects of ability grouping on pupils' developing sense of themselves, their attitudes towards school and their social relationships.

The impact of ability grouping on pupils' self-perceptions

During the early years of primary school, pupils generally have positive views of themselves and their abilities. As they progress through years 3 to 6 they begin to perceive distinctive differences in themselves in relation to their academic, social and physical selves. As they reach the end of primary school and move into secondary school, their perceptions of themselves become less positive (Blatchford 1997; Marsh 1990). Not surprisingly, high-attaining children's views of their own abilities tend to be more positive than those of lower-attaining children. These differences are apparent as early as year 3. However, the differences between the overall self-concept of higher- and lower-attaining pupils are less than those of their academic self-concept (Chapman 1988). This is because overall self-concept is influenced by children's views of themselves in relation to other aspects of their lives such as sport, social relationships and physical appearance.

The effects of ability grouping on pupils' self-perceptions are not entirely clear. International reviews have found no overall effect of ability grouping on self-esteem (Kulik 1991; Kulik & Kulik 1992). When pupils of different levels of attainment have been considered, ability grouping has tended to raise the self-esteem scores of lower-ability pupils and reduce the self-esteem of the higher-ability students. This suggests that streaming and setting might have a levelling effect, with the more able children losing some of their self-assurance when they are placed in classes with children of similar ability. Considering the effects of within-class groupings, Lou *et al.* (1996) reported that pupils in classes where the teacher adopted within-class grouping (either ability or mixed-ability), had more positive views of themselves when compared with those in ungrouped classes. However, Devine (1993) found that the self-image of pupils of average and high ability remained similar regardless of type of grouping (sets or mixed-ability) but only 3 per cent of pupils in low-ability groups held a high self-image compared with 29 per cent of similar ability pupils in mixed-ability groups. As in the case of attainment, the effects of different kinds of grouping on pupils' self-esteem may be mediated by other factors, in this case school ethos and the attitudes of teachers and peers.

Pupil attitudes, expectations and relationships

Early UK studies of streaming in primary schools indicated that social adjustment, social attitudes and attitudes to peers of different ability were 'healthier' among children in non-streamed classes (Willig 1963; Barker Lunn 1970). Streaming had a stronger impact on lower-ability pupils, who had more negative attitudes in streamed schools, whereas the attitudes of high-ability pupils were similar regardless of school type (Barker Lunn 1970, Ferri 1971).

Pupils' attitudes towards school may be influenced by their teacher's attitudes towards ability grouping. Barker Lunn (1970) identified teachers as 'streamers' if they were in favour of streaming and as 'non-streamers' if they were in favour of mixed ability. The poorest attitudes were found among pupils in non-streamed schools who were taught by teachers who were streamers. Boys of below average ability had the most favourable relationships with typical non-streamer teachers in non-streamed schools. The more streams, the more negative the attitudes of those in the lower streams and the greater the possibility of them regarding themselves as stigmatised (Barker Lunn 1970). Children of below-average ability who were taught by teachers who preferred streaming but worked in non-streamed schools were friendless or neglected by others. Their teacher's emphasis on academic success and dislike of the below-average pupil may have been communicated to other pupils who, in turn, rejected the below-average child. Rudd (1956) reported that streamed children made fewer contributions and paid less attention in lessons. Their behaviour was also more aggressive than that of non-streamed children. There is very little research on the influence of setting on primary school pupils' attitudes, although one study found that setting also had a negative impact on pupils in low groups (Devine 1993).

The extent to which pupils participate in school activities is also an indicator of their attitudes towards school. Barker Lunn (1970) found greater participation among children in non-streamed classes, particularly among those of average or below-average ability.

Parents' expectations are also shaped on the basis of their child's stream. Barker Lunn (1970) surveyed parents' expectations and revealed that parents took their child's stream to be an indication of their future prospects. Where schools did not stream, the links between the ability of the child and parental aspirations were less close.

Effects on social mixing and cohesion

Those advocating mixed-ability grouping and comprehensive schooling suggest that these can have important benefits for society in promoting social mixing among pupils. As we will see in Chapter 3, this is a view shared by primary school pupils themselves. However, when it comes to choosing friends, it seems that primary school pupils tend to select those of similar social class, ability and ethnic grouping regardless of the grouping arrangements in the school (Barker Lunn 1970), although more social mixing occurs where pupils are not ability grouped. The recent adoption of setting procedures, where pupils regroup for different subjects as they progress through school, can split friendship groups and reduce the social support that pupils have developed. Some pupils report anxiety when groupings change and they have to work with different pupils and fit into new structures (Chaplain 1996).

It has been suggested that mixed-ability teaching can lead to greater social cohesion because pupils help each other and the more able provide encouragement and support for the less able by their example (DES 1978; Scottish Office 1996). As we shall see in Chapter 3, this is a view expressed by the pupils themselves. However, observing the teaching of 9–11 year olds, Peverett (1994) found little evidence that lower-ability pupils benefited from the presence or support of higher-ability pupils and studies in the USA have reported that pupils enjoy lessons more when they are grouped with others of similar ability (Kulik & Kulik 1982). These mixed findings may reflect cultural and school ethos factors.

Some studies have indicated that there are qualitative differences in peer interactions in low- and high-ability groups. Behaviour is often more disruptive in the lower sets whereas in mixed-ability classes lower-ability pupils tend to behave better (Slavin & Karweit 1985). Slavin and Karweit have argued that this is because every class has a norm for appropriate behaviour. Mixed-ability classes are likely to have higher morale and place a higher value on learning than bottom sets or streams.

The relationship between ability grouping and social cohesion within the school as a whole is complex. Jackson (1964) found more cooperative atmospheres in non-streamed schools. As we shall see in Chapter 3, where setting is adopted in primary schools it can legitimise the differential treatment of pupils and those in both the lower or higher sets can become the targets of teasing. The more the school highlights differences between pupils in different groups the greater the likelihood that this may occur (Ireson & Hallam 2001). Similarly within the classroom, teachers who draw attention to ability groups make them more salient for pupils (MacIntyre & Ireson 2002).

Social consequences of ability grouping

When streaming was widely adopted in the UK, there was clear evidence that the low streams tended to include disproportionate numbers of pupils of low socio-economic status, boys and those born in the summer (Douglas 1964; Barker Lunn 1970). More recently it has been demonstrated that pupils in certain ethnic groups are over-represented in low sets in some secondary schools (Gillborn & Youdell 2000). Allocation to groups is not solely on the basis of ability and many different factors influence the groupings that are formed in schools and classrooms. As we shall see in Chapters 2, 3 and 5, these include social relationships between pupils, gender and behaviour, physical aspects of the classroom and class size. Some pupils exhibiting poor behaviour are placed in low groups irrespective of their level of attainment. In other cases, teachers deliberately split up groups of potentially disruptive pupils into different ability groups in order to be better able to control their behaviour. This can lead to group allocation that is inappropriate in terms of the child's academic attainment (MacIntyre & Ireson 2002). The evidence suggests that pupils make more progress if they are placed in higher streams, compared with pupils of similar attainment placed in lower streams (Barker Lunn 1970). Once pupils are placed in ability groups there is little movement between them. Even within-class groups may be regrouped infrequently, leaving pupils in an inappropriate group. This issue will be explored in greater depth in Chapter 6.

Summary

Ability grouping may have effects on the social and personal development of primary-aged pupils. Children of lower socio-economic status, boys and children born in the summer are likely to be placed in lower-ability groups and, given the relative lack of movement between structured ability groups, remain there. While the effects on self-esteem and social mixing are not clear, pupils in mixed-ability classes seem to hold more favourable attitudes towards school. Mixed-ability classes avoid the stigmatisation of those in the lower streams, although teacher attitudes and school ethos factors appear to have mediating effects. These issues will be explored more fully in Chapters 3, 4 and 5.

Conclusion

The evidence presented in this chapter suggests that structured ability grouping, of itself, does not raise levels of attainment. Neither does it have consistent effects on pupil self-esteem because academic self-concept constitutes only one part of overall self-perception. Highly structured ability grouping may be socially divisive, in that particular groups of pupils are consistently allocated to the lower-ability groups. These pupils may be stigmatised as a result of their group placement. Mixed-ability grouping appears to promote more positive attitudes towards school among those of lower levels of attainment. As movement between structured ability groups is infrequent, once allocated to a group, pupils tend to remain in it. As allocation to groups is often made on grounds other than prior attainment this has important implications for equal opportunities and social justice. Within-class groupings appear to be beneficial in raising achievement but their success depends on the way that they are implemented in the classroom. In particular, the quality of teaching and the way that groupings are aligned with particular teaching objectives needs to be carefully considered. These issues will be addressed in more detail in later chapters.

Chapter summary: ability grouping in primary schools

Historically, the extent to which structured ability grouping has been adopted in UK primary schools has depended on political priorities and educational thinking at the time.

During the 1990s schools came under increasing pressure to adopt the practice of setting.

Research on the effects of streaming and setting has revealed that there are no consistent effects on pupil attainment or self-esteem.

Allocation of pupils to ability groups is based on a range of factors, not only prior attainment.

Movement between groups is limited.

Some groups of pupils are more likely to be allocated to the lower-ability groups.

When structured groupings are adopted lower-ability pupils may be stigmatised, higher-ability pupils may be teased.

These effects may be mediated by school ethos, the nature of the curriculum and the quality of the teaching.

Further reading

Hallam, S. (2002) *Ability grouping in schools: a literature review*. London: Institute of Education, University of London.

Ireson, J. & Hallam, S. (2001) *Ability grouping in education*. London: Sage.

Sukhnandan, L. & Lee, B. (1998) *Streaming, setting and grouping by ability: a review of the literature*. Slough: NFER.

Chapter 2

Making decisions about grouping practices

Introduction

Historically, schools have been free to make their own decisions about the kinds of pupil grouping that they adopt, although from time to time they have been under considerable political pressure to adopt particular practices. Whether schools choose to follow government guidance depends on a wide range of factors. In this chapter we will outline what considerations influence schools' decisions about grouping, including those relating to raising academic standards, meeting non-academic needs, practical issues, school ethos and accountability. First, we will provide a brief overview of what is known about the grouping practices most commonly adopted in schools.

Current grouping practices in the primary school

In recent years, as we saw in Chapter 1, schools have been under considerable pressure to adopt structured grouping practices, in particular setting. In the mid-1990s, Ofsted began to comment on the organisation of pupils into ability groups (Ofsted 1997) and noted its increase at primary level, especially in years 5 and 6 for mathematics and English (Ofsted 1998a, 2001). A survey established that 60 per cent of junior schools set for at least one subject in some year groups, while over one third of infant schools and about one half of combined infant and junior schools did the same (Ofsted 1998b). The higher the number on roll, the more likely the school was to use setting in one or more year groups. Most schools used setting in years 5 and 6 only, with the proportion of pupils setted for at least one subject falling steadily the younger the pupils were. Of those schools that adopted setting procedures, the proportions that set for particular subjects were: maths, 96 per cent; English, 69 per cent; science, 9 per cent. Very few schools set for other subjects. Overall, the research showed an increasing trend towards adopting structured ability grouping with a move away from within-class ability groups in mixed-ability classes which had previously been the dominant form of grouping (Bealing 1972).

A more recent study (Hallam *et al.* 1999a), based on a sample of 2,000 randomly selected schools, examined differences in grouping practices in schools with same- and mixed-age classes.

Schools with same-age classes

For schools with same-age classes, the most common form of pupil grouping is within-class, either mixed-ability or ability grouped. Only in mathematics and English is there any substantial evidence of setting. Less than two per cent of schools adopt streaming. Setting is most frequently adopted in mathematics and increases as pupils approach national assessment tests in year 6. It is predominantly within year groups although there is some evidence of cross-age setting (see Figure 2.1). In English a similar pattern emerges but, overall, there is less setting (see Figure 2.2). The predominant form of grouping for the remainder of the curriculum is mixed-ability grouping within the class. There is some evidence of ability grouping being adopted for science but this is mainly within-class (see Figure 2.3).

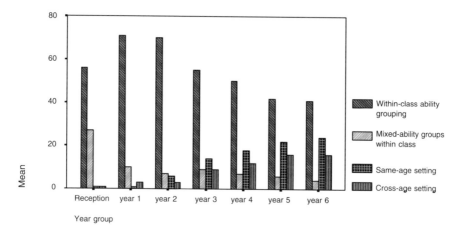

Figure 2.1 Types of grouping adopted in mathematics in primary schools with same-age classes

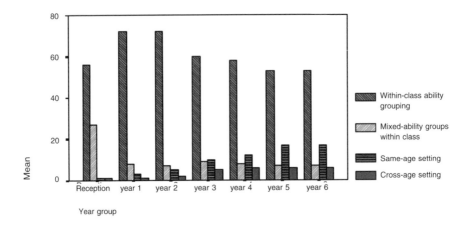

Figure 2.2 Types of grouping adopted in English in primary schools with same-age classes

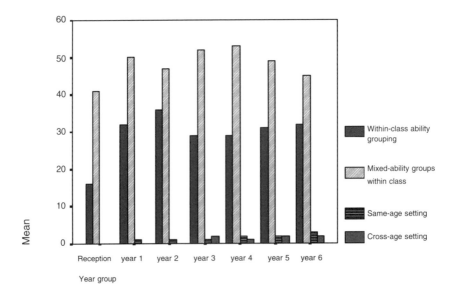

Figure 2.3 Types of grouping adopted in science in primary schools with same-age classes

Schools with mixed-age classes

In schools with mixed-age classes, the overall pattern of grouping is similar to those where classes are of the same age but there are differences relating to same-age and cross-age setting. In maths and English there is a greater proportion of cross-age setting as compared with the schools where classes are the same age. In English the pattern is less consistent than in mathematics (see Figures 2.4 and 2.5).

Changes in pupil grouping

As we have seen, in recent years there has been a trend towards increased structured ability grouping. Why has this occurred? When asked, schools have indicated that changes have been made in response to the literacy hour, the numeracy hour, a combination of these and for a range of other reasons (Hallam *et al.* 1999). Figure 2.6 illustrates the

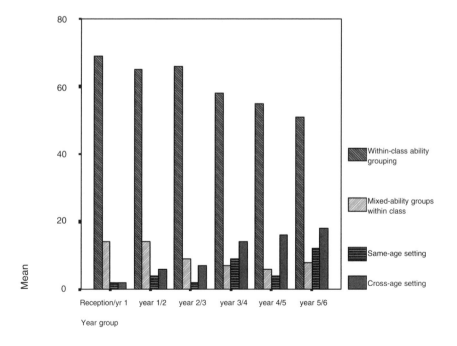

Figure 2.4 Types of grouping adopted in mathematics in primary schools with mixed-age classes

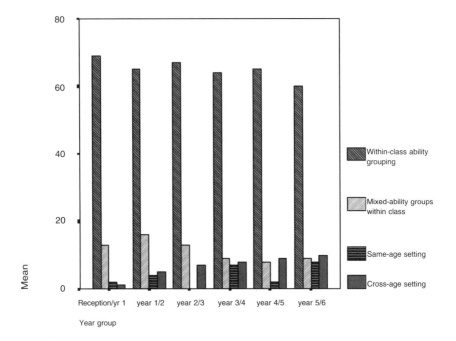

Figure 2.5 Types of grouping adopted in English in primary schools with mixed-age classes

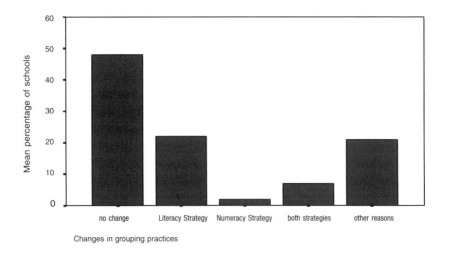

Figure 2.6 Reported reasons for changing grouping practices

proportion of schools indicating change and the reasons for it. The next sections will explore in more detail the factors that influence schools' decisions as to whether to change or retain existing grouping practices.

Why and how schools adopt particular grouping practices

When considering how to group pupils, schools take account of a range of factors. These include:

- raising standards;
- matching work to pupil needs;
- the demands of different curriculum subjects;
- making the best use of teacher expertise;
- the National Literacy and Numeracy Strategies;
- meeting the non-academic needs of pupils;
- school and class size;
- resources;
- timetabling;
- school ethos; and
- accountability to outside bodies (Ireson & Hallam 2001).

The arrival of a new head teacher can also pre-empt change.

Academic considerations in taking decisions about grouping practices

Schools' main consideration when taking decisions about grouping practices is related to pupils' academic achievement and the need to match work to pupil needs.

Raising standards

The single reason why schools most often change grouping practices is to raise standards. This is despite the lack of evidence that structured ability grouping improves performance. For example: 'The change to setting was to try to raise our SATs levels and attainment generally' (400+ on roll, same-aged classes).

In some cases schools have organised groupings specifically to prepare pupils for taking national tests: 'Each year from January until the SATs, year 6 children are ability grouped for weekly sessions in English (writing), maths and science to give them the best opportunity in the SATs and to provide revision' (300–400 on roll, same-age classes).

In making these changes schools are attempting to match teaching to pupil needs to enable each pupil to attain their full potential.

Meeting pupil needs

Grouping pupils by ability enables a reduction in the amount of differentiation of work needed within each class: 'Setting provides a narrower band of intellectual ability to cope with, making differentiation more manageable' (200–300 on roll, same-age classes).

Adopting structured grouping does not remove the need for differentiation within classes but can reduce its range. The difficulty is deciding at what point the extent of difference in prior attainment necessitates pupils being taught separately rather than differentiation occurring within the class through within-class ability grouping, differentiated tasks, assessment or questioning. This decision may be influenced by the proportion of children with Special Educational Needs within each class, those with English as their second language or other groups with particular learning needs. For example:

> Most of the pupils speak EAL (85 per cent) and 150 pupils are on the SEN register. Many speak little or no English. Therefore by setting we can improve the offer made to children of all abilities. The teaching is more focused for the ability of the children. Setting reduces the amount of teacher planning needed but even in setting differentiation is essential. (400+ on roll, same-age classes)

Withdrawing children with specific needs

A long-established alternative to setting is to withdraw some children from classes. Historically, this practice has been adopted in relation to children with Special Educational Needs, who have been withdrawn for additional support or special tuition. This practice, while offering the opportunity to match work closely to pupil needs, can stigmatise those who are withdrawn and reduce their opportunities to experience the curriculum shared by the other pupils. An alternative is to provide a timetabled period when pupils undertake a range of activities that meet their specific learning needs. These could range from enrichment activities to those unrelated to academic work, e.g. the development of social skills.

Targeting provision

Another approach to pupil grouping is to target pupils who with additional support are likely to attain higher levels in national tests, particularly those on the borderline between levels 3 and 4. The weakness of this strategy is that it can mean that those children who are perceived to be unable to attain national standards may be neglected. Targets of attainment need to be defined for all children to ensure that they, and their teachers, strive to achieve the highest possible standards of which they are capable.

The practices described in the preceding sections relate to the needs of schools to meet national targets and to perform well in a competitive education system where there is intense public scrutiny of performance tables. Some schools also take account of the demands of different subject domains and attempt to use grouping structures to make the best use of teacher expertise.

Demands of different subject domains

Strategies for grouping pupils can take account of the differential performance of pupils in subjects other than numeracy and literacy and their personal, social and cultural needs. For instance:

> One tries to group to the needs of the child as well as the subject. Some subjects like music, the children are set for skill/concept development for part of a lesson as appropriate. Some subjects for this age group, the benefits gained in the 'hidden curriculum' demand mixed ability even though the skills/thinking may be accelerated by not doing so. (200–300 on roll, mixed-age classes)

> There are times when alternative group patterns are used for a specific purpose (e.g. PE, swimming towards gaining certificates). Other arrangements have to be made for RE as some children are of religious groups and the curriculum has to be dealt with differently for them in some circumstances. (200–300 on roll, same-age classes)

If pupils are grouped across classes, i.e. same- or cross-age setting for most curriculum subjects, substantial amounts of learning time can be lost in the movement of pupils between groups. The strategy may then be counterproductive. Where pupils are taught by different teachers in most curriculum areas, class teachers may have insufficient knowledge of individual pupils' overall progress.

Making the best use of teacher expertise

Historically, high-ability groups in streamed systems have tended to be taught by those teachers perceived as the 'best', usually the more experienced and better qualified. Low streams have tended to be allocated the less experienced and less well-qualified teachers (Jackson 1964; Barker Lunn 1970). Some schools use grouping structures or flexible timetabling arrangements to take advantage of staff expertise. This may mean that teachers specialised in particular curriculum subjects teach that subject to all pupils. This often occurs in relation to music or art. In some subjects, again, the better-qualified teachers with the most experience in the subject may take the highest-attaining pupils. This tends to happen in mathematics. In addition to making the best use of teacher expertise these approaches can also make best use of teacher time. For example:

> We have setting for English and maths in year 3–4 for more efficient delivery of the curriculum, enabling teachers to address the needs of children more effectively. Subject exchanges for PE, music and RE in Key Stage 2 enables use of teacher expertise and more efficient use of teacher time as each teacher plans and delivers one of the three subjects to all three parallel classes. (300–400 on roll, same-age classes)

Making use of teacher expertise to provide all pupils with high-quality learning experiences is clearly desirable. However, allocating the most expert teachers to work consistently with the more able has the disadvantage that it serves to communicate to other pupils that the able are more highly valued. As we will see in Chapter 3, pupils are aware of the way that teachers are allocated to teach particular groups. Indeed, there is a strong case to be made that pupils of lower ability are in greater need of high-quality teaching. Each school has to consider these issues in the light of the particular expertise of its teachers and the extent to which it is practically possible for them to teach different groups of pupils. Large schools, with more teachers, tend to have greater flexibility than schools with one teacher or less for each class.

The National Literacy Strategy

The introduction of the National Literacy Strategy had a major impact on schools' grouping practices. The guidance from the DfEE in relation to the teaching of literacy states that for 75 per cent of the time pupils should be taught together, in mixed-ability classes, while the rest of the time should be spent in group tasks differentiated by prior attainment. Differentiation at the class level is justified in some circumstances, for instance, in classes with more than two year groups or where reception children are taught with years 1 and 2. Some schools have followed this guidance and reorganised their practice to enable single-year groups to be taught together. For example: 'We have changed our practice. Support is given by the head teacher by taking one year group in each Key Stage 2 class in order to teach the literacy hour to a straight year group' (100–200 on roll, mixed-age classes); 'We changed because it was difficult to teach the literacy hour to two year groups and impossible for three' (less than 100 on roll, mixed-age classes).

Other small schools have adopted a different approach and constructed cross-age sets: 'More able children are now working with years 3–4 for literacy and numeracy and the more able year 4 children are now working in the year 5–6 class for literacy and numeracy' (less than 100 on roll, mixed-age classes).

Some large schools have used setting to reduce the range of prior knowledge for the 'whole class' element of the literacy hour, justifying this practice in terms of the class having too wide an ability range.

> We changed our practices because of the demands of the National Curriculum but in particular the literacy hour. Even before the literacy hour we felt that we needed to address the issue of our brightest children possibly through setting. We feel that the literacy hour would be unworkable unless we were putting the children into sets. (300–400 on roll, same-age classes)

In some schools setting was common practice prior to the introduction of the National Literacy Strategy. In these cases, schools have had to make judgements about its benefits. Some have retained setting, others have abandoned it, others have adopted a combination of mixed-ability classes and setting. These decisions have been based on teachers' knowledge of the spread of attainment among the children and the extent to which teaching in ability groups for the whole of the literacy hour will raise attainment for all pupils.

The DfEE guidance suggests that pupils should be ability grouped for some elements of the literacy hour. This allows pupils to benefit from whole-class teaching which ensures that there is similar coverage of the curriculum by all pupils, that expectations remain high for those who are at lower levels of attainment and that lower attaining pupils are provided with positive role models. The work in ability groups facilitates specific targeting of work for the practice and development of particular skills. As pupils approach national testing at Key Stage 2, schools are more likely to adopt ability grouping practices during the whole of the literacy hour in preparation for the tests, particularly where pupils in different year groups are taught together. This enables work to be provided for year 6 pupils that focuses exclusively on test preparation.

In some schools the implementation of the literacy hour has led to changes in grouping practices in other curriculum areas. The grouping structures adopted for the literacy hour are maintained across subjects. The advantage of this is that it simplifies classroom management. However, this may be detrimental to overall pupil achievement as pupils tend to perform at different levels in numeracy and literacy. If work is to be set to meet pupil needs, allocating them to the same group for both is likely to be ineffective. In some cases, the introduction of the literacy and numeracy strategies has led schools to reconsider the make up of existing ability groups to take account of attainment in different subject areas.

The National Numeracy Strategy

The guidance provided by the DfEE regarding the National Numeracy Strategy acknowledges that setting for mathematics has been in place in some schools for a considerable length of time. However, it does not endorse setting, suggesting that 'as standards improve over time, the range of attainment in each year group ought to reduce so that it becomes possible to cater for the diversity of needs by grouping pupils within the same class' (1999: 20). This constitutes a clear indication to schools that setting is not recommended within the numeracy hour.

Use of grouping strategies to satisfy non-academic aims

The purposes of adopting particular grouping practices can go beyond those related to academic attainment. Groupings can be used as a way of managing behaviour and facilitating the development of a range of social and personal skills.

Improving behaviour

The reasons given for adopting particular grouping practices are in some cases related to managing difficult behaviour. Groupings can be used to split up pupils who demonstrate challenging behaviour or to ensure that pupils work well together. While this strategy can be easy to manage within classes, when groupings are across classes, unless the school is very large and has a series of parallel groups, it can be difficult to organise successfully and pupils are often placed in groups that do not relate to their levels of attainment.

Promoting personal and social development

Particular within-class groupings can be used to promote the development of particular social and transferable skills. For example:

> We aim to promote collaboration and not competition and therefore find that children work better in small groups that have clear, concise guidelines and where all children have a particular task to complete. (100–200 on roll, same-age classes)

> Children are grouped in various ways so that they have the opportunity to develop skills of negotiation, cooperation and adaptability. They need to work in different groups to develop these skills. (less than 100 on roll, mixed-age classes)

Group work can be used as a means of giving additional responsibility to more able children. For example:

> Sometimes in English and maths the children may be put together in mixed-ability groups if the teacher wants children to work together without adult support, e.g. a capable child taking the role of scribe in a literacy group activity. (200–300 on roll, mixed-age classes)

Pupils can benefit from working collaboratively in mixed-ability groups as this can develop independence and cooperative behaviour.

> We changed our grouping practices from ability grouping to mixed-ability grouping after staff training in 1997 on the more able child and encouraging independence for all children. Some classes in year 1 at the time adopted ability grouping for mathematics. At the same

time we implemented the literacy hour and teachers found that it helped their teaching to have the children in mixed-ability groups especially at year 2 level. Children were able to support each other. There was no slow or poorly motivated group that needed all the teacher's input and teachers found that they were freed up to support each teaching group in turn. All children seemed to benefit, the less able as well as the able, and SATs results went up to reinforce the benefit. (200–300 on roll, same-age classes)

Although different types of grouping can be used to promote the development of a range of personal and social skills, overall the overwhelming emphasis in organising groupings in schools is on raising academic standards. The extent to which schools are able to implement particular groupings to this end depends on a range of practical issues. It is to these that we now turn.

Practical considerations

School and class size

Key factors in the implementation of different grouping practices are the size of year cohort and school. Many schools have intakes that do not fit into acceptable class sizes. This creates particular difficulties for small schools. While large schools may face similar problems they have more flexibility in resolving them. Difficulties relating to class size can change from year to year and in some cases within a year for reception classes. This can make long-term planning difficult.

Problems of small schools

For small schools, particularly where there are three or more year groups in one class, the organisation of pupils into groups to provide optimal learning opportunities for children is a constant cause for concern. Very small schools are rarely in a position to provide same-age tuition for all the children and cross-age grouping is common. Sometimes this is based on ability. This is not without problems. For example:

We have ability groups now for English, although in a whole key stage class it is important to be sensitive, e.g. not year 3 and year 6 together even if they are the same ability because needs are different.

Also we have a high proportion of children on the SEN register stages 1–4 so we use grouping to scaffold and support SEN children who may be working with the more able children to raise achievement and expectations. (less than 100 on roll, mixed-age classes)

More able children are now working with years 3–4 for literacy and numeracy and the more able year 4 children are now working in the year 5–6 class for literacy and numeracy. The school needs to be flexible with grouping practices because of the small intake of pupils in each year. The grouping practices may change in future years. (less than 100 on roll, mixed-age classes)

In these and similar circumstances, grouping strategies have to be constantly reviewed to provide the best possible support for pupil learning.

Mixed-age classes

Mixed-age classes pose particular problems because the National Curriculum and systems of testing are year based. This problem is not restricted to small schools. Generally, schools and teachers prefer to have same-age classes. Teachers find that teaching and planning work for single-year classes is easier, although some schools do use ability rather than age to determine class membership. This sometimes gives parents cause for concern, particularly where they feel that their child is being held back by being in a class with younger pupils. Overall, schools need to adopt a wide range of solutions to maximise opportunities for pupils' needs to be met in order to raise standards. In addition to school and class size, resources are important in the kinds of grouping arrangements that schools are able to adopt.

Resources

A constraint for schools in deciding on particular grouping practices is funding for staffing. Whatever their aspirations, if funding is not available then plans may not come to fruition. Structured-ability grouping inevitably means that more staff are required. If two classes are combined and split into three sets then an additional teacher is required and additional accommodation. Where classrooms are not available, creating additional sets is not practical. Timetabling difficulties linked with resource issues can also limit opportunities to adopt particular grouping structures. For example:

> Setting has ended in this academic year. For the last two years we had mixed-age classes in Key Stage 2. Maths setting was in operation in Key Stage 2. Classroom assistants are now used to improve differentiation within single-aged classes. Setting was considered for this year in maths but the timetabling strictures of the literacy hour were a major factor in deciding against it. (200–300 on roll, same-age classes)

As the previous sections have described, decisions taken by schools relating to the way pupils are grouped tend not to be based on ideology. The main reasons for schools adopting particular grouping practices relate to raising standards, in particular performance on national tests, and to meeting the learning needs of pupils. The extent to which schools are able to implement their preferred grouping structures depends on resources, staff and accommodation.

School ethos

While decisions about pupil grouping, in most cases, are underpinned by pragmatism rather than ideology, the type of grouping structures adopted do impact on school ethos. The term ethos is usually adopted to describe the overall feel, style or climate of a school. The factors that contribute to this include pupil and teacher morale; teachers' job satisfaction and the degree to which they value teaching as a profession; the degree to which the school is seen as a safe, comfortable and pleasant environment for work and leisure; the learning context; teacher–pupil relationships; issues of equality and justice; extra-curricular activities; school leadership; discipline; information to parents; and the extent of parent–teacher consultation (Scottish Education Department 1992). Pupil grouping, in the way it affects pupils' personal and social development, and influences pedagogical practices and the relationships between pupils and teachers, is therefore a factor in determining school ethos.

When streaming was commonplace in the UK, it was based on the assumption that ability was largely inherited and therefore immutable (Jackson 1964). Within streamed schools, this led to prejudice against and the stigmatisation of pupils of below-average ability. Streamed schools tended to be systematic in their educational approach, concentrated on the 3Rs, made extensive use of tests, were supportive of streaming and had authoritarian teachers. In contrast, unstreamed schools were more relaxed, had less individual work and a less competitive atmosphere. Teachers were more permissive, preferred more active methods of instruction, emphasised self expression and personal experience and were critical of tests, selection and streaming. There was a greater union in the objectives of teachers in the streamed schools and a tendency for many teachers in non-streamed schools to hold attitudes or implement policies at variance with the stated policy of the school. These factors influenced the development of certain school-related attitudes in the pupils and the motivation to do well in school in children of average and below-average ability. The children in non-streamed schools held more favourable attitudes than pupils in streamed schools, they also participated more in school activities, although in both kinds of school the more able children and those from the higher social classes tended to be more committed (Barker Lunn 1970).

The current educational climate in the UK, with its emphasis on raising standards, rigorous and frequent school inspections, the publication of national test results and the competition between schools to attract high-attaining pupils has reduced the opportunities for schools to exhibit diversity in their educational approach. The educational aims included in school documentation are remarkably similar, although in practice there can be substantive differences in the way these aims are operationalised (Hallam et al. 1999). The written aims of primary schools tend to focus on enabling each child to develop to his or her full potential academically, personally and socially, although these aims may be pursued through very different grouping strategies: combinations of streaming, setting and within-class ability or mixed-ability grouping. These impact on pupils in very different ways which will be explored in detail in Chapter 3. Grouping structures, while they do not define school ethos, play a role in shaping shared attitudes within the school which in some cases value some pupils more than others. Examples of the written aims and teachers' and governors' interpretations of them, taken from three schools adopting contrasting grouping practices, are given in boxes 2.1 to 2.3. The first section in each box sets out the aims as written in the school prospectus. The second section gives examples of the way that staff interpreted the aims in a series of interviews.

In school 1, despite written aims that express a balance between academic, personal and social educational outcomes, teachers emphasise academic performance. The school is committed to structured ability

School 1: A very large grant-maintained suburban school. Children are assessed on entrance to the school and are streamed according to ability in Key Stage 1 and year 3 for the whole curriculum. In Key Stage 2, from year 4, pupils are organised into mixed-ability classes and are set for the core National Curriculum subjects. Specialist teachers work with higher-ability sets.

Written aims as set out in the school prospectus:

The educational philosophy of this school is based upon the view that every child should be regarded and valued as an individual person with academic potential, needs, problems and aspirations, who can make a distinct contribution to the life of the school. This school will provide a stimulating and exciting learning environment in which children are able to learn, create and experience, and to display their achievements. Parents, pupils and staff, in cooperation, will create an atmosphere to which the child will respond by accepting responsibility for his behaviour, his work and his attitude to the community's needs. The children will be encouraged to have an understanding, sympathy and tolerance for cultures and societies other than their own.

School aims as perceived by the staff:

The children come first each and every time. We are 'results-driven' I think but the children are happy with that – we're not doing anything that makes the children unhappy. I think that by streaming them, we'd get those results easier than if we didn't stream them. I had concerns that we were working very hard and very fast, and at a very high level with young children. And I think that one of the reasons that I am teaching in that class, in the A stream, is that I know – I can see the signs when children are becoming unhappy. I know then that I'm working them too hard and I know what to do when that happens and I can make them happy. I know that through experience because the first year that I had a year 2 A class, I was distressed because they were becoming distressed and I knew that I had to get through this huge amount of work and get these results, and I didn't quite know how to do it at the time – it was just work, work, work, and during that year I learnt an awful lot about how to keep them happy and how to make it not seem like such hard work. I don't think that they [the grouping practices] detract from the aims at all, they enhance them in many ways. Not just their learning but their social groups as well . . . they get a lot from each other. Perhaps the A stream do get more, but as I've said the top of the B classes is so similar that all children are going to get a similar mix. (Key Stage 1 teacher)

Our aims are to be the best really and to do the best for the children and to give them every chance to succeed. I think that the setting does that . . . When I first came I was really shocked by it. I had all these ideas that the children should all be together, I was really into mixed-ability teaching, but when you're here, you just see that this system works. (Key Stage 2 teacher)

Box 2.1   School aims and their operationalisation in a school adopting streaming and setting

School 2: A very small rural school where pupils are arranged into two mixed-age class groups according to key stage, and are subsequently grouped in a wide variety of ways, including some setting, according to the curriculum area, teacher judgement, and available space.

Written aims as set out in the school prospectus:

It is the aim of the school to provide the building blocks necessary to empower children with the skills they will need, to provide educational and enrichment activities that will enable them to achieve their individual potential and become responsible citizens. We aim to:

- Provide a solid background in the core subjects and do all we can to help our children achieve in these areas;
- Provide many experiences for hands-on instruction in mathematics, science, communications and computer technology, recognising that these are the areas where children will be competing for jobs in the future;
- Provide an atmosphere where children are taught responsibility and are held accountable for their achievement and for the choices they make;
- Teach social and cooperative skills needed to lead a successful life;
- Recognise that children will be the leaders of tomorrow;
- Recognise that children, teachers, and the whole school community grow in an environment of positive reinforcement where all are encouraged to better themselves.

We believe our school is a warm caring place where children feel comfortable and happy about their learning. Some of the beliefs that we as educators hold about children are:

- They are unique and important. All children can and will learn and each requires differing amounts of time and practice.
- The most successful children are those whose parents play an active role in their education.
- Positive motivation strategies maximise learning opportunities.
- Self-esteem is at the heart of successful, happy children.

School aims as perceived by the staff:

That each child is seen as a whole person and that we have the academic as well, and we have to push them. I've got a little girl in my class at the moment who's an extremely good reader but socially she's not astute at all, and we're trying to address that problem to make sure that when she moves through the school she's got friends, because otherwise she's going to finish up just being on her own and that's not a good thing for her nor for anyone else. The whole of the time, the idea is to keep in your mind that this child is different to every other child and we've got to address this child's needs. (Head teacher)

That the children are happy and that when they enter, who knows where they've been beforehand, but when they leave the school, you want them to be confident, happy as I said, and able to cope with the next step of their education, whether it be the local secondary or, I don't know, a private boarding school. We want them to be able to cope with what life throws at them next. (School governor)

I'd like to think that we create an environment for children to learn in and that we give out comfort and support and help, but also that our expectations of the children are quite high and that their expectations of themselves should be quite high as well because we have got some very bright kids and I think that we do let them know that we think that they do very well. (Key Stage 2 teacher)

Box 2.2   School aims and their operationalisation in a school adopting flexible setting

School 3: A large inner city school with children organised into same-age, mixed-ability class groups. The school has no formal policies on ability grouping or setting. For some subjects, particularly maths, children are ability grouped within a mixed-ability context.

Written aims as set out in the school prospectus:

The aims of the school are:

- To encourage a calm, secure, purposeful and happy atmosphere within the school, to enable children to work to the best of their ability, showing interest and enthusiasm.
- To foster positive caring attitudes towards everyone where academic and social achievements at all levels are acknowledged and valued.
- To encourage increasing independence and self-discipline so that each child learns to accept responsibility for her/his own behaviour.
- To have a consistent approach to behaviour throughout the school with parental cooperation and involvement.
- To trust children and teach them to be honest and trusting with each other and to develop their respect, kindness and consideration of others.
- To raise awareness about appropriate behaviour by making boundaries of acceptable behaviour clear and to ensure safety.
- To create an environment where teachers, children, parents and other adults alike can expect to be listened to and treated politely and fairly.
- To respect children's individuality when responding to their behaviour and encouraging them to think about their behaviour and self-control.
- To create a successful community, the individuality of all members must be respected, regardless of race, gender, class, religion or differences of a physical nature.

School aims as perceived by the staff:

We concentrate on a moral thing, a teamwork thing – getting the children working together as a team, supporting each other. So there's very much a moral and ethical emphasis within the general aims – in the playground, how to treat each other fairly and all the rest of it. I think we aim to be a very caring school. (School governor)

Well, I think that's probably where it all comes from – that people feel a philosophical commitment to mixed-ability and cross-curricular work as being that which fosters cooperation and everyone working hard at their own level, and praised for what they achieve individually or how they work together, rather than praise because they're the best in a group or class. I think as well that there's a commitment to not drawing attention to the differences in ability. If you set or stream and you have your lists up where you have your groups or your colours or whatever, basically even if we do that, it won't be made an issue. (Deputy head)

The way in which groupings support the aims is perhaps about social integration, developing as a person, as a social being, and having the right and being equipped to speak and all that stuff . . . I think it does support that . . . (Head teacher)

Box 2.3 School aims and their operationalisation in a school adopting mixed-ability teaching

grouping as a means to help pupils attain their full potential and the emphasis, as expressed by the teachers, is on 'results' and wanting to be 'the best'. The statements from the staff and governors in school 2, a very small rural school, indicate that the balance between the academic, personal and social aims set out in the written documentation is actively pursued within the school on a day-to-day basis. School 3, in its written aims, is also committed to enabling all pupils to attain their full potential. However, staff emphasise the commitment to mixed-ability teaching and engendering a supportive and collaborative working environment. This in part reflects the perceived need by staff to promote cooperation between an ethnically diverse intake.

The examples given above illustrate how the nature of the grouping structures adopted by a school reflects the ethos shared by the staff and, as we shall see in Chapter 3, the values that are communicated to the pupils. In taking decisions about grouping structures, schools need to be aware that the adoption of particular types of grouping structures has a very powerful effect on the way that staff approach their teaching, the expectations that they have of different groups of pupils, the nature of interactions between pupils and between pupils and staff and, as we will see in Chapter 4, the actual teaching methods that are implemented. The ethos of the school is affected by the grouping practices adopted. Decisions need to be taken with this in mind.

The role of the head teacher

The head teacher plays a key role in developing policies that satisfy school aims and are commensurate with the needs of pupils and teachers, while also satisfying the demands of governors, parents and the various bodies to whom schools are accountable at local and national level. Head teachers, particularly when new to a school, may feel the need to make changes to a range of current practices including those relating to grouping. For example, as the head teacher of a large junior school where classes were same-age, mixed-ability with setting for mathematics and a year 6 able children's extension group described:

> Well, when I first came here, the head teacher had retired on ill health grounds and there had been an acting head for some time. It was known as a very formal school. It was also known as a school where parents were not welcome into the school, and so it was very much the school did what they thought was appropriate. It's in an area that's regarded very much as 'middle-class professional' and when I came here the school was very strictly streamed. The governors invited me to an open meeting so that I could speak to parents and they could meet me, and it all went really well and everything was very amicable until some of the parents said, 'You will continue the practice of streaming, won't you?' I said, 'I don't think so.' From what I'd seen, I wasn't happy with what was going on. The parents were appalled to think that I wasn't going to carry on with streaming but, anyway, we worked through it. I changed it straight away because I felt that the children in the lower streams had had quite a difficult time because they'd had quite a lot of supply teachers and they weren't really moving on very well. The children in the top streams had always had the most experienced teachers and it just wasn't equality of opportunity at all and so we moved away from that to mixed-ability groups, and I looked at the children that we had, and what we could do with them. We have a lot of high-ability children, but we also have some very complex children with special needs – every sort of syndrome that you could think of – and we also, at the time, had a lot of teachers who were dissatisfied

because they always taught the lower streams. I looked at them and thought, you know, they'd lost their spark, so we needed to address that, and that's what we did. We mixed them all up, regrouped everything – it took a lot of working with parents, getting them in to show them what we were doing. (Head teacher, school 4)

This example shows that a committed head teacher can bring about change even when there is considerable opposition. It also indicates the extent to which there can be parental pressure in relation to the grouping of pupils. This may be in relation to school policy or when individual pupils are moved between sets or groups. This issue will be discussed in more detail in Chapters 3 and 6.

Accountability

Schools, as represented by their head teachers, are accountable to the governors of the school, LEA inspectors, Ofsted and, because of the market economy in education, as we saw above, parents. Ofsted inspections and their outcomes can provide the impetus for change in grouping policies. For example:

The school was a failing school when I came, so the reputation of the school was rock bottom. It was the school you didn't go to. So I spent a lot of time trying to change the reputation of the school. With the Ofsted report it became apparent that something really needed to be done, and we decided to go down the route of ability grouping. (400+ pupils on roll, same-age classes)

Criticism or advice from outside bodies provides a further source of evidence to be considered when decisions are made about grouping structures. In some cases, where schools are labelled as 'failing', they may have little choice but to implement strategies suggested by others.

Evidence-based decision making

As we have seen, decisions about grouping policies have tended to be driven by the national priority to raise standards and for individual schools to perform well in comparison with others in national league tables. The actual grouping strategies adopted by any individual school are mediated by factors relating to class and cohort size, and available resources. In making decisions about whether grouping strategies are working effectively, schools use evidence from a variety of sources:

> Since the introduction of the National Curriculum, we have gone round in circles at least three times and we have now decided we are going to class teach and cater for special-ability children with differentiated tasks and this seems to be working. We got an excellent Ofsted report last year and the Key Stage 1 and 2 SATs have been 100% level 2 and level 4 with quite a few level 3s at Key Stage 1 and level 5s at Key Stage 2. We do not intend allowing the national literacy or numeracy hour to impinge on us. (100–200 on roll, mixed-age classes)

Adopting an evidence-based approach enables schools to be more systematic in developing policy and practice. Collection of appropriate data enables decisions to be made and rationally justified to external bodies. It can lead to existing practices being retained or new practices being adopted. For example: 'We set during 1996–8 for maths and English in years 5 and 6 but found that it was not justified in relation to the time taken and children's progress, especially children with SEN whose scores seemed to be depressed' (300–400 on roll, same-age classes); 'We used to set across the year groups in Key Stage 2 for maths, English and science. The results did not improve and the lowest ability groups were very difficult to manage' (300–400 on roll, mixed-age classes).

An evidence-based approach enables a range of factors to be taken into account when decisions are made: 'We have found that focusing on set work has had a beneficial effect on children's attainment but there are problems and issues associated with this; movement of pupils between sets; time slippage between one lesson starting and another ending; loss of some other areas of the curriculum' (200–300 on roll, mixed-age classes); 'We did try setting at Key Stage 2 in maths, English and science but found that children didn't have sufficient contact with their own class teacher. We also found that English was best on a mixed-ability basis' (400+ on roll, same-age classes).

In taking decisions about grouping strategies, schools, in consultation with all staff, need to:

- Examine performance indicators for particular groups of pupils in relation to the performance of other similar schools and targets set;

- Explore the reasons for any need for improvement as they relate to pupil grouping;
- Set out an ideal model for the grouping of pupils;
- Examine the feasibility of this given current staffing, accommodation and resources;
- Explore the possible impact of the proposed structures on different groups of pupils' personal and social development;
- Consider other possible drawbacks, e.g. time spent moving between groups, disruption of pupil support for each other;
- Agree a feasible plan;
- Set up systems and a time scale for monitoring its effectiveness; and
- Implement the plan.

If schools take decisions systematically in this way they are likely to optimise the academic, personal and social learning outcomes of all pupils. Decisions based on 'gut feelings' rather than hard evidence about the grouping strategies that are best for raising standards have been shown to be inadequate (Ireson & Hallam 2001; Hallam 2002).

Conclusion

Given the unique nature of each school community and its circumstances it is not possible to provide a simple recipe for grouping practices that will automatically raise pupil performance. Each school needs to evaluate its practice in the light of evidence. This can be derived from a range of sources which may include performance on national tests, pupil progress over time and inspection data. Schools may also have particular concerns that they wish to address. For example:

> The grouping arrangements vary somewhat in the foundation subjects, sometimes friendship, sometimes ability, sometimes gender mixes. We're concerned about boys' standards and the feminisation of the National Curriculum. We're looking at more gender mixing and encouraging reflective thinking. We're concerned that middle sets lose out and we also see the advantage/reality of proximal learning. (200–300 on roll, mixed-age classes)

In addition, schools need to take account of pupils' personal and social development. These are not assessed in national tests and are therefore more difficult to monitor. They are, however, equally important in ensuring the well-being of all pupils as we shall see in the next chapter.

Chapter summary: making decisions about grouping practices

Most primary schools in the UK teach pupils in mixed-ability classes.

Within-class ability grouping is the most common form of grouping in mathematics and English.

Mixed-ability groups are the most common for all other subjects.

The main reasons that schools report for adopting structured ability grouping are to raise standards and meet pupils' learning needs.

Schools are constrained in making decisions about pupil grouping by school size, the make up of year cohorts, staffing, accommodation and resources.

Decisions made about grouping practices need to balance the needs of pupils and teachers and satisfy the demands of governors, LEAs, Ofsted and parents.

The unique nature of each school and its circumstances preclude the imposition of a national policy on grouping practices.

Schools need to continuously monitor and evaluate their practices utilising a range of evidence and make changes as necessary to meet current needs.

Further reading

MacGilchrist, B., Myers, K. & Reed, J. (1997) *The intelligent school.* London: Paul Chapman Publishing.

Chapter 3

Pupils' experiences of different kinds of grouping

Introduction

The effectiveness of the grouping practices adopted in any school can only be assessed in relation to their impact on the learning outcomes of the pupils. These can be considered in purely academic terms or may take account of pupils' personal and social development. While there may be advantages for teachers or for school managers when particular grouping practices are adopted, the key consideration in evaluating success has to be the benefit for pupils. In Chapter 1 we reviewed the literature on the effects of different kinds of grouping on pupils' academic success and demonstrated that no particular grouping structure, of itself, consistently led to improved attainment. We also explored the effects on pupils' personal and social development and showed that where structured ability grouping was adopted there was a tendency for pupils in low-ability groups to become stigmatised and develop more negative attitudes towards school, although some of the claims for enhanced social integration in mixed-ability classes were not supported by the evidence. In this chapter we will consider the reported experiences of low-, average- and high-ability primary school pupils when different types of groupings are adopted in their school. We will explore:

- the extent to which pupils are aware of the grouping practices adopted;
- the reasons they give for those procedures being adopted;
- what they perceive to be the strengths and weaknesses of structured ability groupings;
- the extent to which they see it being possible to change groups;
- what they perceive as the benefits of mixed-ability teaching;
- the extent to which they are aware of teachers' perceptions of their ability;

- the extent to which grouping practices influence teasing of the more and less able; and
- the effects on pupils' attitudes towards school.

It is important that teachers have knowledge of pupils' experiences in school as it provides a means of informally assessing aspects of pupils' personal and social development within the context of current school policies and practices, or what Snyder (1971) called the hidden curriculum. Such knowledge can assist teachers in understanding what pupils have learned about themselves and their place in society from their experiences at school. Much of what pupils learn at school is not part of the academic curriculum. They learn by observing the behaviour and treatment of others; from their interactions with teachers, other school staff and peers; and from the kind of work they are given to do and the way that teachers respond to it. In this way, the values of the school and its staff are communicated to the pupils.

The effects of ability grouping on pupils' personal and social development

As we saw in Chapter 1, the evidence suggests that pupils enter school with generally positive views of themselves which decrease as they progress through the primary years into secondary school. High-attaining pupils have more positive views of their academic ability than low-attaining pupils but overall self-esteem is not always affected by academic achievement as it takes account of other aspects of pupils' lives, e.g. sport, social activities. The effects of ability grouping on academic self-esteem are not clear. While there is some indication that ability grouping may have a levelling effect on self-esteem, lowering that of high achievers and raising that of lower achievers, not all the evidence supports this. As self-esteem depends, in part, on our perceptions of the way others perceive us, the role of significant others in our lives is crucial to its development. The way that teachers interact with pupils of different abilities and the messages that they communicate regarding the value they place on each individual will be crucial mediating factors in the relationship between ability group placement and pupil self-esteem.

When streaming was commonplace in UK primary schools, the social adjustment, social attitudes and attitudes towards peers of different ability were healthier in children in non-streamed classes. Streaming had particularly negative effects on lower-ability pupils. Where teachers valued high academic attainment, pupils of lower ability were stigmatised. Lower-ability pupils taught in mixed-ability classes were more involved in school and had more positive attitudes than those in streamed classes. Pupils tended to choose friends who were of similar ability and socio-economic status to themselves regardless of grouping practices, while claims of increased pupil-helping behaviour in mixed-ability classes were not consistently supported by the evidence. School ethos and teacher behaviour may be important mediators in relation to these aspects of social development. The extent to which these findings apply to setting as opposed to streaming is not clear.

Pupils' experiences of different kinds of grouping

A recent approach to examining the effects of ability grouping on pupils' personal and social development has been to ask them directly about their experiences. Using questionnaires and interviews, Devine (1993) explored primary pupils' experiences of within-class ability grouping for reading. When asked about their preferred group, most pupils said they would least like to be in the lowest group (74 per cent) while 60 per cent wanted to be in the highest group because it gave them status and a feeling of superiority. The pupils were aware that different kinds of activities were undertaken in the different groups. Those in the highest group were most satisfied with the activities that they undertook, while 54 per cent of those in the lowest group expressed dissatisfaction. Apart from those pupils in the top reading groups, most pupils preferred whole class or individual reading to group work. The main reason given for this was that these methods did not leave them feeling left out.

We explored the experiences of pupils of above-average, average and below-average ability in years 3 to 6 attending six primary schools adopting different grouping practices (see Table 3.1 for school details). The pupils were asked questions regarding:

- their attitudes towards school;
- how they were grouped during classes;
- why they thought they were grouped in that way;
- whether the work of the groups was different;

- what they thought were the advantages and disadvantages of particular grouping structures;
- whether they were happy in their allocated group(s);
- whether they would like to change groups and, if so, why;
- how they would set up groups if they had the opportunity;
- whether they were teased because of being in a particular group; and
- what group they thought they would be in if the teacher allocated pupils to one of three ability groups: top, middle or bottom.

Table 3.1   The grouping practices of participating schools

School 1: A very large suburban school with same-age classes. Children are assessed on entrance to the school and are streamed according to ability in Key Stage 1 (KS 1) and year 3 for the whole curriculum. In KS 2 from year 4, pupils are organised into mixed-ability classes and are set for the core National Curriculum subjects. Specialist teachers are employed to work with higher-ability sets.

School 2: A large primary school with classes organised on a mixed-age basis. At KS 1, pupils are in mixed-ability classes with within-class ability groups for the core subjects. At KS 2, pupils are streamed into 3 mixed-age classes based on ability.

School 3: A large primary school where children are organised in mixed-age classes from year 1. Pupils are set for mathematics and English from years 1–2. The rest of the curriculum is taught in mixed-ability or within-class ability groups. There is a KS 2 able children's extension group that receives extra support for one hour a week.

School 4: A large grant-maintained junior school with pupils organised into same-age, mixed-ability class groups. There is setting for mathematics, with the rest of the curriculum taught in mixed-ability groups with some within-class ability grouping. Pupils take the 11 plus selection exam, and there is a year 6 able children's extension group.

School 5: A small rural school where pupils are arranged into 2 mixed-age classes according to key stage, and are subsequently grouped in a wide variety of ways, including some setting, according to the curriculum area, teacher judgement, and available space.

School 6: A large inner-city primary school with children organised into same-age, mixed-ability class groups. For some subjects, particularly mathematics, children are ability grouped within a mixed-ability context, although generally there is a strong commitment to mixed-ability teaching.

Pupils' awareness of grouping structures within the school

The majority of pupils were aware of the grouping structures in their school. The younger respondents in school 1 tended to be unaware of the streaming implemented up to year 3, although children in the top stream knew that they were expected to work at a faster pace and higher level than their peers. Apart from this, most pupils were aware of how and why they were grouped and many of their responses gave rationales for the grouping practices that reflected those provided by the teachers. Where structured groupings were the norm in the school, the pupils referred to the need to match work to pupil needs. For example:

> I think they decided to do that so that the children could get the best education that they need. Then the teachers who are good at different subjects can help the children who need it – they can help the children who are good at something and the children who are different. I think that I prefer setting because I know that with the setting I will be given the best education that I need because when we were doing it as a whole class there were some children who had different abilities from us and the teacher sometimes needed to help them more. During the setting, they mainly focus on your actual ability so the work is really suited to what you can do. It's better when everyone is about the same because then you don't waste your time. (Pupil, school 1)

> One's the smartest class, one's the middle class and one's the slowest class. (Pupil, school 2)

In school 6, where the emphasis was on working cooperatively in groups, the rationales given by the pupils were markedly different to those in the other schools.

> Working in a group you can get ideas from other people and some people work together.

> I think it might be because a lot of people need help with their maths and some of the cleverer people and some of the less advantaged people are put together so that they can help each other.

Where setting was adopted, pupils were very aware of the differences in work that was being undertaken by different sets. For example:

> At lunch times sometimes they're talking about what they do and the rest of us are sitting there and we haven't even heard of the sums. (Pupil, school 4)

> Sometimes when we come in there's something still on the board for maths top set and I just think, oh dear, I don't know how to do that. (Pupil, school 4)

They were very aware of the role of national testing in the adoption of particular grouping procedures:

> It's for the SATs . . . they want to see who's clever . . . they don't want to put everyone in one set because it will be too hard for some people. (Pupil, school 1)

While the details of ability or other grouping structures may not be made explicit to pupils, they are aware of them, are socialised into them and accept the rationales offered by school staff. Where these relate to work being set at an appropriate level, the pupils interpret their group placement as being indicative of their ability. This may lead to a decrease in their motivation, place a limit on their academic expectations and, unless they have strengths in other areas, decrease their self-esteem.

The advantages of setting and streaming as perceived by pupils

The main advantage of setting as perceived by pupils is that work is set at an appropriate level. This view was expressed by 27 per cent of the pupils. Thirteen per cent indicated that setting provided opportunities to work with different pupils, 10 per cent indicated that it enabled better teaching and explanations from teachers and 8 per cent said that when classes were set, the work was at a harder level. Other advantages, relatively infrequently mentioned, included having opportunities to work with other teachers, having the opportunity to gain status by being in a high group, having the opportunity to get a higher grade in national tests and not being held back by other pupils. Very few pupils responded to questions about streaming. Of the responses made, most raised the issue of work being set at an appropriate level.

Work being set at an appropriate level

The main advantage of setting as perceived by pupils is the way it enables work to be matched to their needs. This was raised by pupils at varying levels of attainment:

> I like the sets because you get work that's right for you. (Pupil, below-average ability, school 1)

> It's the bottom set but to tell you the truth I wouldn't want to be in the middle set because I think I couldn't do it. (Pupil, below-average ability, school 1)

Related to this was the question of being held back by being with people who were unable to proceed at the same pace.

> In mixed-ability groups people might be holding you back. You just couldn't get on with your work like you could if it was people of your ability. (Pupil, above-average ability, school 3)

Pupils raised two issues in relation to the matching of work to needs: understanding and pace of work.

> When he goes over things I understand it better . . . I think it's a really good way to work because if we didn't have sets then people who don't understand the hard sums say in maths well they'll get confused and they need something easier so it's better to be in a group that you know that is right for your brain. (Pupil, average ability, school 1)

More frequently mentioned than understanding was the pace of work. Pupils felt that sets allowed them to work at a speed commensurate with their ability.

> Because some people can't learn as fast as us so they have to put them in a slower group to learn things. (Pupil, above-average ability, school 3)

> Some people do get far ahead but we start off on the same page . . .
> in maths it's the same as English, it depends how fast you work . . .
> we start on the same page and then some people might do two pages
> and some people might do three pages. (Pupil, average ability,
> school 5)

When talking about ability grouping within the class pupils raised
similar issues about the pace of work. They commented that having
within-class ability groups saved time and avoided repetition:

> There are three different groups – red, blue and green. Blue is the
> middle, green is the hardest and red is easiest. The teacher decides
> who is in which group by how they can spell . . . and what kinds of
> words they can spell. Teachers put us in the groups so that they
> don't have to spend so much time . . . for example she wouldn't give
> silent letters on the first Monday to people in the blue group and she
> wouldn't give three letter words on the first day to people in the
> green. We might get 5 or even 6 letter words. (Pupil, school 4)

From the pupils' perspective, the main reason for grouping pupils by
ability, either in sets or within class is to match work to their needs so as
to facilitate understanding, enable pupils to work at the fastest pace
possible and save teacher time. Overall, pupils generally felt that the
ways in which they were grouped were effective and most pupils (55 per
cent) indicated that they would not make any changes to the practices
adopted in their school, although there was considerable variation
between schools.

Perceived disadvantages of setting and streaming

The main disadvantages of setting as perceived by the pupils are the
teasing of pupils in the lower (23 per cent) and higher (5 per cent) sets.
For example:

> Science is mixed ability. I think it's nice to have mixed ability
> because it's different and it's nice for the people that aren't very
> good and they think 'oh yea, I feel a lot more comfortable', I expect.
> It's much more fair because then people don't make fun of them
> because they're in a lower group. We would prefer to do maths
> and English like that as well because you get split up – you're not

with your nearest friends and people sometimes tease you that you're in the top group and so it's nice to be with your friends. (Pupil, school 3)

The key disadvantages of streaming are seen as not being in the same stream as friends, the work being too easy, the top streams having more interesting work and being of higher status and the pressures of being in the top stream. Other infrequently mentioned disadvantages include the low status of the bottom stream, teasing related to being in a lower stream and pupils' abilities in different subjects not being catered for.

Reasons for preferring mixed-ability groupings

The main reasons given for preferring mixed-ability groupings related to the ways that pupils could help, inspire and motivate each other. Pupils made direct reference to the way that they support each other in their learning.

Working in a group you can get ideas from other people and some people work together. (Pupil, school 6)

I like working as a group because if you're stuck on something you can ask who's sitting next to you and they can help you out. (Pupil, school 3)

Does it help to work as a group? Yes, because if you get two children, you have double brain power. (Pupil, school 2)

Not all pupils enjoy working in groups all of the time and some groups are clearly dysfunctional.

Once I was with a group and I couldn't get my sums right and nobody would help me and I didn't know how to do them, but I was too frightened that if I said something I would get into trouble, so I just sat staring at my work. (Pupil, school 3)

I've had to work before with a group in year 3 when they didn't actually let me speak – they left me out and just put their own ideas in and when I tried to speak they just spoke over me. I told the teacher and she told them to let me join in. (Pupil, school 4)

Teachers need to set very clear ground rules for pupils when they are working in groups. Children, like adults, do not automatically work well together and need a framework setting out what behaviour is acceptable. This issue will be considered more fully in Chapter 5. There is also a danger that the more able pupils may come to feel that they are shouldering an unacceptable burden in supporting less able pupils. For example:

> Sometimes when people ask me for help I just want to say no because sometimes I just want to get on with my own work. Sometimes when we've finished she might tell us to go and help someone who's having problems. Sometimes it's hard when they still don't understand when you've explained it, especially when it's because they're not listening to you. It might help you to understand better yourself having to explain it and it helps you to get along with other people. But sometimes it's a bit annoying but I like working as a group because you get to know other people and it's a bit more fun because every person has different ideas. (Pupil, school 6)

Closely related to the issue of helping each other is that of social inclusion and the opportunities that mixed-ability grouping provide for getting to know pupils from a range of backgrounds.

> Because it's helping you to work with other people as well . . . if you have to do a science project or a DT project then you have to work with other people even people you don't like that much which helps you to learn a lot about them. (Pupil, school 3)

The perceptions that pupils hold about the strengths of adopting mixed-ability groups within the classroom are, as we shall see in Chapter 5, identical to those put forward by their teachers. Pupils recognise that they can help each other and draw on each other's ideas. Nevertheless, it is clear that pupils require guidance on working together to avoid the development of dysfunctional groups.

Behaviour

Behaviour is an important issue in relation to how pupils are grouped between and within classes. Pupils' descriptions of how they are grouped and seated within the class and how they might group pupils themselves acknowledge the importance of good behaviour and the teacher's use of groupings to help achieve it. For example:

> I'd put the brainy ones not near me but where I could still see them and the people who don't act their age and they do know a lot but they don't get on with it . . . they'd be near me so if they don't get on with it I could tell them off. (Pupil, school 4)

> Some people at the front don't concentrate so Sir has to keep an eye on them at the front . . . that's how he gets them to concentrate. (Pupil, school 2)

Groupings are perceived to have a role in ensuring that children work well together and spend time on task. The manipulation of groups within the classroom is seen as a way for the teacher to reduce class conflict and promote optimum working relationships.

> I think that she looks at who gets on well and will work well together. (Pupil, school 2)

> We stay on the same table groups all the time unless we don't get on very well then the teacher might move us. (Pupil, school 2)

Mixed-gender groups are viewed as one way in which teachers can maintain an optimal working climate.

> I'd let them pick and see if they got on and then I'd probably put boy, girl, boy, girl . . . I'd only do that if they were naughty though. (Pupil, school 2)

> I think that boys can get silly with boys and the girls might be more sensible so I'd put some of the girls with the boys. (Pupil, school 3)

Many pupils are aware of the complex factors which their teachers take into account when allocating pupils to within-class groups.

> I would have them in twos . . . I wouldn't put good friends together because they'd be talking too much but I wouldn't put two people together who hated each other . . . I'd have people who know each other but are not really friendly . . . I would have someone who's not so clever and someone who's clever but if I had two people who

were both really good at say history then I'd swap the class around a bit . . . I'd have different pairs for different things, I think. (Pupil, school 1)

I'd let them pick where they wanted to sit for two weeks and see how they are and if they're not getting on with their mates I'd move them around on tables . . . I'd have a table of year 6s on their own and a table of year 5s on their own and then the rest can be mixed . . . because you might get some people who would mess around so you should try them out with a different year 5 or year 6 and see if they was alright with that. (Pupil, school 2)

Pupils are aware of the importance of behaviour in determining the allocation of pupils to within-class groupings. They demonstrate knowledge of the ways that teachers plan groupings and the factors that they take into consideration. This knowledge is rarely made explicit in schools and is acquired through observation and the informal interactions that take place on a daily basis between pupils and teachers.

Pupils' desire to change groups

Most pupils (55 per cent) reported being happy with their group placement. There were substantial differences between the schools but these were not related in any systematic way to grouping structures. Just over 25 per cent of pupils indicated that they would like to move into a different group to do harder work, while 12 per cent wanted to move groups to be with their friends. Only 2 per cent overall wished to be in a lower group or to have easier work. These children tended to be in the schools with higher levels of streaming and setting. In the school where mixed-ability teaching was the norm most pupils did not want to change groups (86 per cent). In the school where there was cross-age setting the main reason for wishing to change groups was to be with friends. Table 3.2 gives the details.

The single main reason for wishing to change groups was to have harder work. For example:

I find my set a bit too easy. I wouldn't mind being in the middle but not the top. (Pupil, below-average ability, school 1)

Table 3.2   Pupils' desire to change groups

School	Wish to move to a higher group/have harder work	Wish to be with friends	Wish to move to a lower group/ have easier work	Wish to move to be with a particular teacher	No desire to change groups/ happy with group
1	35%	6%	6%	6%	47%
2	21%	17%	4%	4%	58%
3	30%	20%	10%	10%	30%
4	33%	0%	6%	6%	61%
5	11%	33%	0%	0%	56%
6	14%	0%	0%	0%	86%
Total percentage of all pupils	26%	12%	2%	5%	55%

> I'd like to be in a higher science set. I'd like some harder work . . . in my set we have to do things like colouring in and sticking and tests and stuff but it's really easy. I want to get more brainy and go higher. I'd be delighted if they put me in a higher set. I wouldn't mind doing harder work. (Pupil, below-average ability, school 1)

Only two per cent overall wanted to move down to a lower group because the work was too difficult.

> Well, we don't just work out sums and work from a book – we find out problems and we have to work out all these problems and we have to work all these problems out in a different way and, some-times, I wish that I could be in the middle set because it gets a bit too hard. (Pupil, high ability, school 4)

> I'd like to be in a different literacy group. I'd like to go in one that was a bit easier. (Pupil, high ability, school 3)

When pupils are allocated to ability groups, work is not always well matched to pupil needs. Some pupils find it too easy, others too difficult, although most pupils wanted work that was more challenging, suggesting that teachers may underestimate their pupils' capabilities.

Overall 12 per cent of pupils wanted to move group or stay in the same group because of friendships.

> I'd like to be in a different set for English because all my friends are in a different set and I feel left out. (Pupil, school 1)

> Last year I wished I was on a table with my friends. I'm usually with J and that's really good because we like to help each other with things because we're not used to each other sitting together and helping each other so sometimes when I'm not with J it's a bit funny because I'm used to her helping me and me helping her and stuff. (Pupil, school 6)

Being unable to work with friends can have a negative impact either leading to feelings of isolation or removing active support for the pupils concerned. The gender of within-class groups is an issue for a number of pupils, particularly boys. For example:

> Once I was on a table with all girls and I didn't like any of them and I had to sit there for a whole year. So that wasn't very nice. (Pupil, school 6)

> Actually this year I wasn't very happy with my English group because I was the only boy and they're not really my friends. (Pupil, school 5)

Group allocation through gender can lead to boys feeling isolated and unhappy. Some pupils' set preference is influenced by the teacher. For example:

> I would like to be in a higher set but I like the teacher I have. (Pupil, school 4)

Just over half of the pupils taking part in the research were happy with their grouping placement. This proportion varied between the schools but was not related in any systematic way to the grouping systems adopted. The main reason for pupils wishing to move groups was to have harder work. This suggests that teachers may underestimate the capabilities of their pupils, particularly those in the lower-ability groups and fail to set them work that is sufficiently challenging. The second main reason given for wanting to move groups related to friendships.

Pupils perceived that teachers organised groups to promote good behaviour and concentrated working and that sometimes this required friendship groups to be split. For some pupils this created a sense of isolation, particularly for boys placed in all-girl groups.

Perceptions of allocation to and changing groups

Pupils are aware of why they are allocated to particular ability groups.

> They have tests and if your test is level with the bottom set work then you go to the bottom set and if your test result is medium then you go to the middle set and if you got every single one right then you go to the top set. (Pupil, school 1)

They perceive that it is possible to change ability group either within class or between sets and know that this depends on their work.

> They look at your work and what you've done in the year and sometimes people work faster than others so they move up a group. (Pupil, school 3)

> It depends how clever you are and if you can't cope with one group then you can move down to another. (Pupil, school 6)

Movement between groups is not always seen as easy.

> They wait until you get really good before you go to a higher group. (Pupil, school 3)

The perceived role of parents in changing groups

Parents can be influential in pupil allocation to groups or in the way that they move between groups.

> Do children move from group to group very much? No . . . but sometimes if their mum or dad think that they're in the wrong class then they might move to another class or another school. (Pupil, school 2)

My dad talked to the headmistress as well and they moved me up and I felt pleased because I wasn't with the people that I didn't like very much and I felt that I was moving up to my level. (Pupil, school 3)

Teachers are very aware of parental pressure in relation to pupil grouping and, as we shall see in Chapter 6, schools need to ensure that they have detailed information about pupil work when discussing grouping changes with parents.

Teasing

Pupils can be teased about their perceived academic ability. Forty per cent reported being teased or having observed teasing. Some interpreted the teasing as 'playful', but many found it upsetting. Pupils of high ability were as likely to be the victims of teasing as those of low ability. For example:

Sometimes with the top maths set, people do tease you and call you 'boff'. That happens quite a lot. (Pupil, above-average ability, school 4)

I get teased and called the professor because I'm one of the cleverer ones. It bothers me. (Pupil, above-average ability, school 6)

They call us goody-goodies and whiz kids and stuff like that, brainies, as well. Does it bother you? A little bit – I just ignore them and walk away but it does get on my nerves. (Pupil, above-average ability, school 3)

The teasing of pupils in the higher-ability groups is a new phenomenon. When streaming was commonplace it was the lower-ability pupils who were stigmatised. This has continued.

I don't like it when people poke fun. It doesn't happen that often – not quite a lot, but a couple of weeks ago, people laughed at me and sometimes they call you thick. (Pupil, below-average ability, school 1)

People say like 'You're silly' and all that . . . it makes me feel sad. (Pupil, below-average ability, school 1)

People are nasty to me – not everybody, my mates stick up for me. People say 'you're in the lowest class' and stuff like that. (Pupil, below-average ability, school 2)

In some cases the teasing goes beyond verbal abuse and pupils are physically harassed. For example:

Sometimes they say 'you're crap'. Sometimes at play time though they keep tapping on your shoulder and I feel like banging their heads on a brick wall. (Pupil, below-average ability, school 3)

I get teased a lot at the bottom end of the school, I get beaten up and kicked. They throw pebbles and sand at me and call me fatso and all that. (Pupil, below-average ability, school 4)

There were differences between schools in the level of teasing reported. School 5 had a markedly lower incidence of teasing (only 19 per cent), although the children were aware of the ability groupings in place. This suggests that ability grouping is not the only relevant factor. School size, ethos, expectations and the attitudes of parents and teachers may all be important. There was a tendency for teasing to focus on children of different ability in different schools. In school 1, no child of above-average ability reported being teased, whereas 43 per cent of average ability and 57 per cent of below-average had been the target of teasing. The reverse pattern occurred in school 6, which had a commitment to mixed-ability teaching. In this school, 50 per cent of the above-average ability group reported being teased, 37 per cent of the average ability group and only 13 per cent of the low-ability group. Teasing about ability appears to be related to the grouping practices adopted and the values espoused within the school. Table 3.3 provides details of the percentage of children teased in each school.

Awareness of differences in ability

Where pupils are placed in ability groupings between or within classes, they are made more aware of the differences between them. Although there has been an assumption among adults that pupils are aware of the ability pecking order whether classes are mixed ability or set,

Table 3.3 Frequency of teasing by ability

School	Above-average ability	Average ability	Below-average ability
1	0%	43%	57%
2	27%	27%	43%
3	25%	25%	50%
4	25%	42%	33%
5	50%	50%	0%
6	50%	37%	13%
Overall percentage of all children	28%	36%	36%

the evidence suggests that while they may be aware of differences they are not always aware of their extent. In our study, we asked the children to assess themselves academically. This revealed that while the majority of pupils demonstrated a self-perception in accordance with that of their teachers, there were differences between schools ranging from 52 per cent to 76 per cent. The most accurate estimates were made in the school with the greatest degree of streaming and setting. The least accurate were made in the school which adopted mixed-ability teaching in Key Stage 1 and streaming for the whole curriculum in years 3 to 6. In this school 52 per cent of the pupils gave an accurate estimation, 13 per cent underestimated their ability and 35 per cent overestimated. In the school that was committed to mixed-ability teaching, 66 per cent of pupils gave accurate estimations, but with one exception the lower-ability pupils overestimated their ability. This overestimation continued throughout the age range into year 6. Of those who overestimated their ability 64 per cent were boys in comparison with 36 per cent of girls. Of those who underestimated their ability the greatest proportion were girls (55 per cent). Structured ability grouping, which makes visible perceived differences in ability, enables pupils to more clearly identify their place in the pecking order. Where pupils are taken out of classes or move to different rooms for setting procedures the groupings become apparent to everyone. The status of the child in relation to ability is clearly established.

Perceptions of structured groupings as legitimising the differences between pupils

Where structured ability grouping is adopted, it legitimises the differential treatment of pupils in relation to their ability. It acknowledges that there are differences in ability and that it is acceptable to treat pupils with different abilities in different ways, which carry advantages for some pupils.

> In our old class the teachers used to put the clever ones in a higher group and that was a bit upsetting because you knew that you weren't going to go in there . . . I won't say the thick ones but the ones that weren't so clever we were in a lower group and that made you feel uncomfortable . . . I think they should be mixed . . . half the clever people and half the not so clever people so that then you don't feel upset. (Pupil, school 6)

The unspoken values behind ability grouping as perceived by the pupils emerged in subtle ways. One young pupil described how she would allocate pupils to groups:

> I'd put people in groups and the not very clever ones could be a darker colour and the clever ones could be a brighter colour. (Pupil, school 4)

It seems that young pupils internalise the values of the school, accepting what they are told and learning from what they observe. They subsequently make value judgements about the importance and status of ability. This has consequences for those who exhibit extremely high or low attainment. In schools where academic attainment is valued above all else, those of low attainment are likely to be stigmatised. In schools where the emphasis is on inclusion, those of high ability may be teased. The differences between schools in the levels of teasing experienced suggest that teachers can mediate these effects to ensure that all pupils are equally valued.

Effects of ability grouping on pupils' attitudes towards school

Ability grouping does not seem to have consistent effects on pupils' attitudes towards school. Overall, 71 per cent of the pupils expressed positive attitudes towards their schools, although there was considerable variation (61 to 88 per cent). The main reasons given for liking school related to having lots of friends, being in a friendly environment, enjoying particular subjects, having friendly and helpful teachers and enjoying play time. Only 5 per cent of the pupils, overall, expressed totally negative attitudes, although in one school this rose to 13 per cent. The remaining pupils expressed a mixture of feelings. None of the pupils' reasons for liking or disliking school were related to ability grouping practices. The most commonly expressed reasons for disliking school were it being 'hard work' or disliking activities related to literacy. Some said that school was 'boring', others that they didn't like doing particular subjects, that teachers were annoying or that the playground facilities were inadequate. Some simply said that they didn't like school. Table 3.4 gives a summary of pupils' attitudes to school.

Pupils' main reasons for liking school were related to social factors, i.e. having friends, being in a friendly environment and being with kind people. Overall, 25 per cent of pupils referred to this.

I like it. I've got loads of friends here and if I went anywhere else, I wouldn't know any and I'd probably be a bit nervous. (Pupil, school 3)

I like the atmosphere – it's a really sort of friendly atmosphere. You can really talk to people – it's really good. (Pupil, school 1)

Table 3.4 Pupils' attitudes towards attending school

School	Positive	Negative	Mixed
1	74%	4%	22%
2	70%	13%	17%
3	71%	5%	24%
4	61%	0%	39%
5	88%	4%	8%
6	66%	4%	30%
Overall percentage of all pupils	71%	5%	23%

Having friendly, helpful and good teachers was also commonly cited (16 per cent):

> I like it. They teach very well, I think the teachers here are very good and I like having lessons here. (Pupil, school 4)

> I like the way that the teachers teach you. (Pupil, school 1)

Many pupils indicated that they liked doing particular subjects: maths (19 per cent), literacy (18 per cent), sports and PE (17 per cent), art (11 per cent), science (10 per cent), history (6 per cent), using computers (4 per cent), technology (4 per cent) and playing an instrument (2 per cent). Play time was also important and having opportunities to play outside (14 per cent):

> I enjoy going to maths sets and I enjoy having two small breaks and one long one. (Pupil, school 5)

> There are big playgrounds to play in. It's got nice classrooms and we're lucky because we can play around on the playground and do lots of things. (Pupil, school 4)

Some pupils implied that they liked working (7 per cent).

> It gives you something to do rather than sitting around at home . . . I really like English, maths and creative writing. (Pupil, school 5)

> I like it . . . I have lots of friends and I like to play and do loads of work and stuff like that. (Pupil, school 2)

Negative attitudes towards school were related to not liking doing hard work (5 per cent), not liking particular activities, e.g. literacy (4 per cent), maths (2 per cent), and school being perceived as boring (3 per cent).

> Sometimes class can be a bit boring if you're doing a particular topic and it goes on for ever and ever. (Pupil, school 4)

> We do good stuff here and everything but some of the bad things, at the moment, I don't know why but we're just doing lots of revision – I don't know whether that's part of the curriculum but sometimes it gets a bit boring. (Pupil, school 6)

It is clear that the majority of pupils enjoy going to school because of the social life that it provides and the opportunities that they are given to learn and engage in interesting activities. Grouping structures of themselves do not directly influence attitudes towards school and were not mentioned directly by any of the pupils, although there were large differences in positive attitudes between schools. Table 3.5 summarises pupils' perceptions and attitudes towards grouping practices, school and being teased.

Table 3.5 Pupils' perceptions of and attitudes towards grouping practices, school and being teased

	Awareness of grouping practices, attitudes towards school, learning and teasing
School 1: Streaming at KS1 and in year 3, setting for core curriculum for rest of KS2.	74% of pupils expressed positive attitudes about attending school. The majority were aware of how and why they were ability grouped. This awareness increased with age. Most felt that the ability grouping practice was effective and met their needs. 30% of pupils claimed that they had been teased because of their placement with many of these children being of lower ability. All of them indicated that they found the teasing hurtful. 35% wished to move into a higher group. Over 75% were able to assess themselves accurately in accordance with their teacher's assessment.
School 2: Mixed-ability/within-class ability grouping in KS1, streaming for the whole of the curriculum in KS2.	70% of pupils expressed positive attitudes towards school. The majority of pupils were aware of how their class groups were formed and most were happy with the grouping arrangements within the school. 21% indicated that they would like to be moved into a higher class. 29% of pupils indicated that they had been teased. Most reported that they found this hurtful. Most of these pupils came from the lower-ability classes. 52% of pupils were able to assess themselves accurately academically in accordance with their teacher's assessments.
School 3: Setting for maths and English from year 1. Mixed-ability/within-class ability grouping for the rest of the curriculum.	Over 70% of pupils reported liking school. Most pupils were aware of how their class groups were formed and most were happy with the grouping arrangements. 33% of pupils claimed that they had been teased within the school. The highest proportion of these were the lower-ability pupils. 30% of pupils indicated that they would like to be moved to a higher set or group. 69% of pupils were able to assess themselves accurately in accordance with their teacher's assessment.

Table 3.5 (continued)

	Awareness of grouping practices, attitudes towards school, learning and teasing
School 4: Setting for maths from year 4. Mixed-ability/within-class groupings for the rest of the curriculum.	61% of pupils expressed a positive attitude towards school with the remainder expressing mixed as opposed to negative attitudes. The majority of pupils were aware of how and why they were grouped and felt that it was a good way to work. 61% had no wish to change groups. 52% indicated that they had been teased about their allocation to a group. 75% of these indicated that this teasing was hurtful. 76% of pupils were able to assess themselves accurately in accordance with their teacher's assessment.
School 5: Cross-age setting for maths and English.	88% of pupils expressed positive attitudes towards school. Most had a clear perception of how and why they were grouped in school (generally related to issues of applying themselves to work). Generally, they were accepting of these decisions. Of those wishing to change group the main issue arising was friendship but questions regarding the gender composition of groups also arose. Most did not wish to change groups. Only 8% reported being teased and this was of a playful nature. 70% of pupils were able to assess themselves accurately in accordance with their teacher's assessment.
School 6: No setting. Mixed-ability/within-class grouping.	66% of pupils expressed a positive attitude towards school. Only 4% expressed negative attitudes. The majority of pupils were aware of how and why they were grouped and felt that it was a good way to work, although there was some evidence of the above-average pupils suggesting that they were not stretched enough. 33% of pupils indicated that they were teased because of their allocation to groups, although the majority suggested that the teasing was of a playful nature. 69% of pupils were able to assess themselves accurately in accordance with their teacher's assessment. Many below-average pupils did not consider themselves to be below average.

Conclusion

What can we learn from this study of pupils' experiences of different grouping practices? First, pupils become socialised into the types of grouping structures in their schools and accept the rationales offered by their teachers for those grouping structures. They are able to articulate the advantages and disadvantages of the different types of grouping practices in terms very similar to those adopted by their teachers. They are aware of the ways that their teachers use within-class groupings to improve behaviour and promote concentration on work and of the complexity of factors that teachers take into account when allocating pupils to groups. Mixing the gender of groups is one way that teachers attempt to promote time on task. Girls are generally seen as a calming influence on boys. However, in some cases, boys and girls resent these manipulations. Pupils are aware of the possible benefits of working in groups through supporting and helping each other, but some groups are dysfunctional and some pupils resent having to spend time explaining to others.

Where structured ability groupings are adopted, they legitimise and make more transparent differences in pupils' attainment. Contrary to popular belief, pupils are not entirely aware of the extent of the differences in attainment between them. This is particularly true of the lower-ability boys who tend to overestimate their capabilities when they are in mixed-ability classes where there is little differentiation by ability within the class. In addition, the process by which pupils' level of attainment becomes public through structured grouping leads to teasing of high and low ability pupils which is unpleasant for both. The nature of the language adopted, such as 'thick' or 'dumb', with its negative connotations stigmatises those of lower ability. The greater the extent of the structured groupings the greater the apparent stigmatisation of those in the lower groups. Where there is a strong commitment to mixed-ability teaching, the above-average ability children seem to experience a higher level of teasing. Given these possible negative effects, teachers need to be aware of the messages that they communicate to their pupils about what and who they value and ensure that all pupils are treated equitably.

Pupils' attitudes towards school are not directly related to the type of ability grouping adopted. Most pupils express positive attitudes towards school. What they value most is a warm, caring atmosphere where friendships can flourish and teachers are seen as helpful and supportive. Some pupils are interested in learning particular school subjects and enjoy learning for its own sake, but some perceive school work as boring and express dislike for particular activities. The wide variation in attitudes suggests that schools can create a caring ethos and make school enjoyable regardless of the grouping structures adopted. This is likely to be achieved only where staff at all levels within the school are aware of the effect their actions have on pupils and take conscious decisions to behave in ways that create an appropriate, supportive, learning environment.

Practical implications

In Chapters 4 and 5 we will consider how schools can maximise the effectiveness of different kinds of grouping to promote learning. However, there are steps that schools can take to create a suitable environment for learning regardless of the grouping structures adopted. The social climate of the school is critical in creating such an environment. If children are afraid of being bullied and there is disruption both in and out of lessons, the possibility of effective learning taking place will be considerably reduced. Alternatively, if there is mutual respect, clear communication and well-focused attention to a wide range of different kinds of achievement, the possibilities are great. Schools can assist in this by:

- emphasising, praising and rewarding the positive aspects of the behaviour and work of staff and pupils;
- ensuring that firm and fair action is taken where there is evidence of inappropriate behaviour in pupils or staff;
- setting up mechanisms to allow pupils to seek help and support;
- ensuring that playgrounds are safe environments;
- ensuring that toilet facilities are appropriate, clean and safe;
- providing safe storage for pupils' belongings;
- encouraging all pupils to become involved in after-school and lunch time activities, social occasions, breakfast and homework clubs; and
- paying attention to the quality of personal relationships throughout the school and ensuring that they meet acceptable standards.

While teachers and the adult world in general perceive the purpose of attending school in educational terms, pupils see it as a place to meet friends and have fun. Where children have developed friendships and an enjoyable social life they are more likely to enjoy school, attend regularly and participate actively and enthusiastically in the learning experiences on offer. Where bullying is rife, the social aspects of schooling can become intolerable for some children. Schools have a responsibility to ensure that the environment is safe and supports learning.

Chapter summary: pupils' experiences of different kinds of grouping

Pupils are socialised into the grouping structures adopted in their school and are able to articulate rationales for them that reflect those of their teachers.

Pupils share the same perceptions of the advantages and disadvantages of different types of grouping as their teachers.

Pupils are able to detect when they are being grouped by ability even when they are very young.

Structured ability groupings legitimise differences in pupils' abilities, raise awareness of them and make it acceptable to treat pupils in different ways. This can lead to teasing of the more and less able.

A large proportion of pupils want to move to a different group, most because they perceive the work as too easy.

Pupils' attitudes towards school appear to be unrelated to grouping factors but differences between schools suggest that ethos factors are important.

Schools have a responsibility to ensure that the learning environment is safe and supportive.

Further reading

Rudduck, J., Chaplain, R. & Wallace, G. (1996) *School improvement: what can pupils tell us?* London: David Fulton Publishers.

Chapter 4

Streaming and setting

As we saw in Chapter 1, streaming was, at one time, the norm in those UK primary schools that were large enough to implement it. During the 1960s schools began to change their practices and most classes became mixed-ability. Where ability grouping was adopted it was generally within the class, at the discretion of the class teacher. As part of the effort to raise standards during the 1990s, the DfEE indicated that primary schools should consider setting. Inspections of individual schools and the Chief Inspector's annual reports began to refer to grouping practices and Ofsted commissioned research into the prevalence and implementation of setting. As a result of this, as we saw in Chapter 2, setting increased – particularly in mathematics and English and for pupils preparing for national testing in year 6. Despite this, most schools have retained mixed-ability classes with ability grouping only occurring within the class.

In this chapter we will focus on issues relating to the adoption of structured ability grouping in schools including:

- the arguments for and against structured systems of ability grouping;
- raising standards;
- the effects on pupils' personal development;
- the social implications of structured ability grouping;
- teachers' beliefs and attitudes;
- the National Numeracy Strategy;
- the National Literacy Strategy;
- parental concerns;
- when setting can be beneficial; and
- minimising the negative effects of setting.

The historical arguments for and against structured systems of ability grouping

Interest in the effects of structured ability grouping on pupil attainment and personal and social development has a long history. As early as

1931, Turney outlined what were then perceived as the advantages and disadvantages of systems of streaming. These are set out in Table 4.1.

The observations made by Turney in the 1930s refer to issues that are central to considering the effectiveness of structured ability grouping. However, the demands made on schools have changed considerably since the 1930s. We now have the National Curriculum; pupils are tested at 7, 11 and 14; national literacy and numeracy strategies have been developed and implemented; targets have been set, nationally and at school level, for the raising of standards; and test results are published. Schools are in competition with each other to attract pupils and the views of parents have become increasingly important in determining policies, particularly in relation to controversial issues like ability grouping.

Table 4.1 Advantages and disadvantages of structured ability grouping as outlined by Turney (1931)

Advantages of structured ability groups	Disadvantages of structured ability groups
They permit pupils to make progress commensurate with their abilities.	Slow pupils need the presence of the able students to stimulate them and encourage them.
They make possible an adaption of the technique of instruction to the needs of the group.	A stigma is attached to low sections, operating to discourage the pupils in these sections.
They reduce failures.	
They help to maintain interest and incentive, because bright students are not bored by the participation of the dull.	Teachers are unable, or do not have time, to differentiate the work for different levels of ability.
Slower pupils participate more when not eclipsed by those much brighter.	Teachers object to teaching the slower groups.
They make teaching easier.	
They make possible individual instruction to small slow groups.	

Also important in relation to ability grouping has been the change in attitudes towards children with learning difficulties. There has been formal recognition that some children have Special Educational Needs (SEN). Systems have been set in place that enable pupils with difficulties to be identified, their needs to be assessed and monies to be provided to support their learning. Each school is required to have a special educational needs coordinator (SENCO) and many schools employ teachers or teaching assistants who are trained to work with children with learning difficulties. For those who have chosen to specialise in this area, there is no reluctance to work with the less able. This is a fundamental change since the 1930s.

We will now examine the advantages and disadvantages of structured ability grouping as these apply to raising attainment, pupils' personal and social development and issues for society within the current educational context.

Raising attainment

The evidence set out in Chapter 1 indicated that adopting structured ability grouping, of itself, does not raise attainment. In fact, the most recent evidence suggests that when pupils are taught mathematics using the same curriculum materials, progress is greater in mixed-ability classes than when pupils are taught in sets (Whitburn 2001). Other factors are clearly implicated in improving pupil performance. These include the quality of the teaching, the presence of high-ability role models when all pupils are taught together and pupil motivation and effort. In the next sections we will explore why setting, a practice that should enable all pupils to make the best progress possible as it matches work to pupil needs, does not always succeed.

Matching work to pupil needs

One of the perceived advantages of structured ability grouping is that it enables work to be better matched to pupil needs. Pupils and teachers both acknowledge this. In practice, this means that the more able pupils are stretched or 'pushed'. For example:

> For children particularly at the top, we can stretch them and push them and tell them how wonderful they are, whereas if we had a lot of children together it would be difficult. I think that without the

groupings it would be difficult to create such a positive learning environment. (Key Stage 2 teacher, school 1)

The aims I would say are, in my view, to push children to achieve the highest standards that they are able to achieve and, from that point of view, I think that the grouping practices are successful. (Key Stage 2 teacher, school 1)

In theory, work is also set at an appropriate level for other pupils. For example:

So, how it fits with our ethos is that if children are in a set where the work is appropriate and challenging, the expectation is that they can do it and they will succeed in it. They'll have to work hard, but they can succeed and they will get help if they need it to succeed and when they succeed, they feel good about themselves. That is much better than being stuck in a class with everyone together, with them knowing that they're not really as clever as him or her or them, and therefore deciding to shut up because their opinion is not as valid as the other children's. I've seen that happen, so I think that it works very well with our ethos, because what we're saying is, we're all good at different things, we're all in different sets for different things, the classes are different for different things. There are classes where everyone is together like music and PE, but mostly we're not all together – we're in our group and we can do our best within what we're doing. (Head teacher, school 3)

In practice, however, teachers seem to underestimate the capabilities of pupils who are not in the top set, particularly those in the lowest sets, and the work that they are given is often not sufficiently difficult or challenging for them. The evidence for this comes from the pupils themselves and also, as we shall see later, from observations by Ofsted inspectors who report more poor-quality teaching in lower sets (Ofsted 2001).

Teacher expectations

When schools take decisions to adopt structured ability groupings the expectations of teachers change. These changes in teacher thinking are translated into classroom practice and ultimately communicated to pupils through the everyday interactions that occur in schools.

Teachers have lower expectations of pupils in lower-ability groups so that the work given is less challenging and, as we saw in chapter 3, pupils often perceive it as too easy. In addition, teacher expectations about pupils' capabilities can be communicated to the pupils themselves, who may then come to believe that there are limits to what they can achieve. For example:

> Streaming should create the opportunities for every individual to reach their maximum potential – that was the real philosophy behind doing it, to meet the needs of the children. Well, my personal gut feeling is that we have children who are very keen to learn. I don't feel as yet that we have tapped into their full potential. I feel that the grouping practices in part have assisted children to develop individually but not to their maximum potential and I think that one has to be very careful that the children are being challenged enough. My fear as an adult, is the case of a child saying, 'Well, this is all I'm able to do because I'm in this class or that.' I don't really think as yet that we have an ethos that tells all children that they can succeed. Since I've been here I've had said to me over and over again, 'But it's these children', you know, as if there are limits, and depending on what ability group they're in, their limits are even more limited and I don't see that. (Head teacher, school 2)

As this head teacher acknowledged, allocating pupils to groups based on ability influences teacher expectations which in turn can influence pupil expectations. As we shall see later, there is also evidence that structured ability grouping, in the way it legitimises the differences between pupils, influences parental expectations of their children.

The importance of role models

In addition to influencing expectations, streaming and setting reduce the opportunities for less able pupils to work with and emulate their more able peers. As two staff members indicated:

> I have to say that I see strengths and weaknesses in what we do [streaming] to be honest. I think that it's very advantageous to be grouped by ability so that you can be teaching to the majority and there's no-one who doesn't understand, and no-one being kept back, so I understand that advantage. My main concern would be with the lowest-ability children who are all clumped together because I think

it's very important that children have role models and that they learn from each other and I just worry that if there are children in there who can't learn from . . . who haven't got a model to stretch them if you like, then I think that concerns me. (Key Stage 1 teacher, school 2)

They have to have the role models – if they're all of similar ability, how do they know how far they can fly? (Head teacher, school 2)

In the world of work, it is readily acknowledged that working with people who are more skilled and expert can not only be inspirational but provide opportunities for the individual to learn, develop and enhance their own skills. Apprenticeship is based on these assumptions. These principles apply equally to children. Streaming and excessive use of setting can limit these opportunities.

Effects on the curriculum

Where structured ability grouping is implemented, the activities under-taken in the classrooms of high-, middle- and low-ability pupils differ considerably. There is usually differential access to the curriculum, the top groups benefiting from enhanced opportunities. An informal syllabus often operates where, for the lower-ability groups, topics are omitted and there are different expectations. Differentiated access to the curriculum has been shown to be one of the key factors determining differences in attainment (Creemers 1994). As soon as pupils are put into ability groups the curriculum changes, as does the language that is adopted.

The language development that you can use with the A group . . . you've only got to spend some time sitting listening to the kind of exposition of language that's used for the children that really are buzzing about maths. The curriculum that they're being offered is essentially different. (Deputy head maths coordinator, school 1)

The introduction of the National Curriculum and national testing that is based on pupils attaining different levels seems to have determined the way in which teachers think about the curriculum leading to a concentration on national test 'levels'.

> For my particular area [English] a child in the top set will be comfortably working at level 4 and so the teacher that's working with them will be working on level 5–6 activities. The bottom set – some of those children will be still at level 2 and so the aim of their teacher will be to get level 3 in their SATs at the end of Key Stage 2. So the small group activities will be geared to specific things that will help them to get a level 3, and possibly a level 4 for some of them. The actual activities that the teachers are working on are completely National Curriculum related. (Deputy head teacher, coordinator for English, school 1)

The publication of national test results and competition between schools has increased pressure to ensure that the maximum numbers of pupils achieve high levels, in some cases beyond what is expected nationally. The focus is very much on test performance.

> The A stream get a much higher-level curriculum but also because at the end of Key Stage 1 we're trying to achieve as many level 3s as possible. The time scale is very, very short so by the end of year 1, hopefully they'll have achieved level 1 so that I'm really trying to teach to level 3 more or less in a year. So not only is it a higher level, it's also much quicker as well. (Key Stage 1 teacher, school 1)

This may mean that for some pupils the pace is too fast.

Pace of work

One of the key differences in the teaching of pupils in high- and low-ability groups is the pace of work. Matching pace to the children's needs is perceived to be important.

> By focusing the work to the right level I suppose and making sure that the pace is right and it just works with children of that kind of ability – the way that you can talk and speak to them and how much you can say in your instructions. (Key Stage 2 teacher, school 3)

> The streaming definitely helps – you can work at a fast pace, your teaching can be so much more focused and the children all understand. I think that's got a lot to do with it. (Key Stage 1 teacher, school 1)

In lower streams and sets pupils are given longer to complete work and instructions tend to be shorter.

> I think that you have to give people longer time – shorter instructions – you wouldn't plan to cover so much so quickly with the lower groups really. (Key Stage 2 teacher, school 3)

In addition to the pace of work, ability grouping leads teachers to adapt other aspects of their teaching.

Effects on pedagogy

At secondary level, where ability grouping is commonplace, there is a tendency for instruction in lower-ability groups to have a different quality to that provided for high-ability classes. Observers have noted that instruction is conceptually simplified and proceeds more slowly. There is more structured written work, which leaves work fragmented. Higher-ability classes tend to be set more analytic, critical thinking tasks, particularly in some subjects. Pupils in high-ability groups are also allowed more independence and choice, opportunities are provided for discussion and pupils are allowed to take responsibility for their own work. Low streams tend to undertake work that is more tightly structured. There is a concentration on basic skills, work sheets and repetition with fewer opportunities for independent learning, discussion and activities that promote critique, analysis and creativity (see Sukhnandan & Lee 1998 and Hallam 2002 for reviews). There is a hidden agenda, high-ability pupils being encouraged to work independently and be self-regulating, while for low-ability students the agenda is concerned with conformity, getting along with others, working quietly, improving study habits, punctuality, cooperation and conforming to rules and expectations (Oakes 1985). These differences in instruction may be a means of classroom control, lower-ability groups being perceived as more difficult to manage (Metz 1978; Vanfossen *et al.* 1987).

At primary level, very different activities are undertaken by pupils in different ability groups.

> In the infants, it's that the top-ability group do a lot more reading and writing – it's quite intensive, the amount of work they do – there's a lot of talking about their ideas to me. Then the differentiation between them and the lower end is a more pictorial response

with me scribing the words for them [the lower-ability group] using words banks, using IT to support learning so they have access to a program that they can use so then that frees me to work with someone else. (Head teacher, school 5)

Teachers differentiate the difficulty of the questions that they pose to different groups of children.

Well obviously you'd approach a more able group differently to a less able group. In literacy, certainly during the whole-class teaching, if you're questioning, then you'd set a certain standard of a question and address that to particular individuals in a class. You wouldn't expect to address the same type of question to a lower-ability group so again, the questions and the responses that you expect from the children are guided by your differentiated activities that you ask the child to get involved with. (Key Stage 1 science coordinator, school 2)

Teachers work with the children in different ways. There is a greater emphasis on using games and motivating the pupils in lower-ability groups.

We've got quite a big stretch of resources so that I can highlight things like rhyming games and things that they can do with Mrs P so that I can then work with the high-flyers. In maths, again, it's a similar sort of thing, there are games that they can play, they've got workbooks although I don't let them do the workbooks until we've covered the work in a practical way. (Head teacher, school 5)

There is an expectation that the more able will work independently and the demands made of them are likely to develop a wide range of transferable skills.

The top ones – it's much more problem-solving and investigative work that I give them to do. It's the same in the juniors. The teacher sits with the lower ones at their table very often with maths because the high flyers, once it's been explained to them, are capable of going away and doing it themselves and they might have a hiccup but then they'll just come and ask. Those children that need help really need you there, so that's the way we tend to work. M will sit with his group and S's high flyers will just come if they need you, having had the problem set. (Head teacher, school 5)

Teachers ensure that where pupils are likely to need additional support it is readily available. However, this may encourage dependency in pupils.

Planning lessons and reducing within-class differentiation

Teachers find planning and teaching easier when working with ability groups (Ireson & Hallam 2001). There is also less need to prepare differentiated materials.

> We started setting in year 5–6 about five or six years ago for maths and that was just for those year groups and across the three classes. Instead of grouping within the class, we put them into three sets. We did that because when we were planning, we found that we were all trying to plan a great, large range of work for the children and we were all planning the same thing. We thought that this was crazy – we were trying to rush around and teach, not just manage a class, to teach children, some of whom are at level 5 and some who are still at level 1 or 2. That's what it's like at the top of the school. So, we decided to try setting. (Head teacher, school 3)

The perceived similarity of ability of the pupils enables teachers to focus their teaching.

> The things you can do with the children are different because you've only got children of a certain ability – all the differentiation has been taken away because you can go in and with my top set science for example, I know that they're all working at level 5–6 and so I don't have to have level 3 work ready for certain children . . . we're much more directed and focused. (Key Stage 2 teacher, school 1)

As we saw in Chapter 3, not all of the pupils feel that the work they are given to do when they are grouped by ability is of an appropriate level. Even within ability groups there seems to be a need for some differentiation.

Classroom organisation

When pupils are grouped by ability, teachers tend to adopt a more formal approach with more whole-class teaching. The examples given below illustrate this clearly.

> I'm quite formal. The children sit in rows most of the time. I group them sometimes but for most of the time it's a lot of whole-class teaching rather than group teaching because they are all of a similar ability by the nature of the streaming system, so they can all more or less cope with the same input although I do differentiate at times. (Key Stage 1 teacher, school 1)

> I suppose my teaching style is quite formal . . . whole-class teaching with the class looking at the board or computer screen and that's how it is . . .. In the lower sets not so much because you've only got a few children so we tend to do more practical things and work in that way, but for the higher groups I mean we do experiments and all that but it is much more teacher-led. (Key Stage 2 teacher, school 1)

Whole-class teaching is used less with lower-ability sets who tend to be given more opportunities for practical work. The way that teachers organise their teaching with particular ability groups takes account of the ways that they perceive different pupils learn and engage with learning. Underlying the way teaching is organised are assumptions about concentration, the capacity to work independently and behaviour.

Teacher time and ability grouping

Within a structured ability grouping context teachers indicate that it is easier to allocate their time between pupils. As pupils are seen as working at similar levels teachers perceive that they do not need to spend more time with those who might be experiencing difficulties. Pupil behaviour tends to determine how teacher time is allocated. Teachers acknowledge that this tends to be better in setted rather than mixed-ability classes.

> It's easier in the set than when we're in the mixed-ability class . . . the only times that some children might get more attention is from behaviour problems really, not ability . . . when they're in a set,

you know that all the children can do the work. You might get behaviour problems and it's those children who take up more time, but generally they're better behaved in sets than they are in their mixed-ability classes, so it's easier. (Key Stage 2 teacher, school 1)

I suppose that work is more focused and at their level really . . . in the mixed-ability class, it's the less able children who take up my time. (Key Stage 2 teacher, school 1)

Allocation of resources

Historically, high-ability groups in structured ability systems have tended to be taught by those teachers who were perceived as the 'best', usually the more experienced and better qualified. Low streams have tended to be allocated the less experienced and less well qualified teachers (Barker Lunn 1970). Within the context of streaming and setting, allocating the teachers with the most expertise to the highest-ability groups has been perceived as making the best use of resources as we saw in Chapter 2, but it can also be interpreted as a distribution of resources that favours those who have the least need. For example:

I felt that the children in the lower streams had had quite a difficult time because they'd had quite a lot of supply teachers and they weren't really moving on very well. The children in the top streams had always had the most experienced teachers. (Head teacher, school 4)

The allocation of teacher expertise is a major issue for schools adopting structured ability grouping and one that demonstrates the underlying school ethos. Historically, other scarce resources have tended to be channelled towards high achievers although current provision for pupils with statements of Special Educational Needs has ensured greater equity.

Evidence from Ofsted and DfEE guidance

Although during the early 1990s Ofsted supported setting as a means of meeting the demands of the National Curriculum and raising attainment, recent Ofsted reports have acknowledged that 'Setting does not, by itself, guarantee success in raising standards' (1998b: 5). There is a lack of a clear statistical link between the extent of setting in schools and the attainment of pupils (Ofsted 2001).

The report on the first year of the National Numeracy Strategy echoed the observations of teachers and pupils in our six case study schools (Ofsted 2000b). When setting was adopted, teachers found it easier to teach the narrower range of attainment within a set, there was more whole-class teaching during the main teaching activity, which enabled teachers to maintain a good pace throughout the lesson. Where schools did not adopt setting, teachers reported the value of all pupils, including those with Special Educational Needs, sharing the same mathematical experiences and hearing the same vocabulary. Teachers raised concerns about the disruption that they thought would occur if pupils had to move from room to room. The report also noted that there were no significant differences in the overall quality of teaching between setted or unsetted classes (Ofsted 2000b).

Focusing on the quality of teaching, including careful assessment and close attention to the acquisition of basic skills, was seen as making the clearest difference to pupil attainment. Inspectors reported that quality of teaching in sets tended to be either very good or very poor and was better in the upper sets in mathematics and English, which were often taken by subject coordinators (Ofsted 2001). In mathematics, the least effective teaching was found in the lower sets. Inspectors expressed concern about this given that most schools had introduced setting to raise the attainment of low-attaining pupils. In English and science the weakest teaching was seen in middle sets, where three or more sets had been formed. In English, special educational needs coordinators frequently taught the lower sets.

Guidance on provision for able pupils in literacy and numeracy recognises the advantages and drawbacks of setting, acceleration and within-class support. While setting is seen as allowing a faster pace, the introduction of more challenging materials and tasks, and can make planning easier, there is an emphasis on it being used flexibly with suggestions that it can be used temporarily or part time and that its usefulness depends on how many able children there are in relation to other children. The guidance indicates that it may be more appropriate for older pupils and that where it is adopted there is a need to ensure that low sets have teachers who have a good level of expertise. Introducing acceleration for individual pupils in some subjects may be appropriate but this has the disadvantage of weakening links with the rest of the curriculum as topics will be out of step (DfEE 2000).

Overview

Structured ability grouping, of itself, does not raise standards. While teachers find planning and teaching easier when they are working with pupils of similar levels of attainment this does not always translate into better pupil performance. There are several possible reasons for this. Ability grouping tends to lower expectations for pupils who are not in the highest set. They receive a different curriculum, taught differently, that teachers believe is matched to pupil needs but that pupils, all too often, perceive as too easy and lacking challenge and interest. Grouping pupils by ability reduces access of the less able to parts of the curriculum, high-ability role models and examples of high-quality work which they might emulate.

Personal outcomes of structured ability grouping for pupils

As we saw in earlier chapters, where ability grouping is highly struc- tured and the ethos of the school is such that a high value is placed on academic performance, those in the lower-ability groups can become stigmatised. Where a greater emphasis is placed on mixed-ability grouping, equity and collaboration the more able pupils may be teased. However, it seems that it is not the ability grouping, of itself, that directly leads to these outcomes. Rather it is the ethos within which it is embedded. Structured ability grouping adopted in a limited and flexible fashion, underpinned by a philosophy that genuinely has the best interests of all the pupils at heart, where resources are allocated fairly, where all pupils are valued and this is expressed in the everyday interactions between teachers and pupils, may have no negative con- sequences for the personal development of particular groups of pupils. Some schools have recognised this. For example:

> People come and say, 'Don't children get fed up and depressed and feeling not good about themselves when they're in a low set because they know they're in a lower set?' It's something we debated long and hard at the early stages of setting this up because the ethos of the school is that all the children are important and that a big word is respect – that adults respect children and children respect adults. (Head teacher, school 3)

Unfortunately, these conditions rarely prevail. In most cases the values underpinning ability groupings become part of the fabric of school life and are communicated verbally and non-verbally to the pupils on a day-to-day basis. The way that groupings determine the curriculum and progress through it and the relative lack of movement between groups means that ability groupings made at an early age determine expectations about educational success and ultimately career opportunities.

Social implications of ability grouping

Pupils from some groups are disproportionately represented in the lower groups, summer-born children, those from some ethnic minority groups, and boys (see Sukhnandan & Lee 1998 and Hallam 2002 for reviews). As we shall see in Chapter 6, accurately and fairly placing children into ability groups is difficult and once ability groups have been established movement between them is limited, particularly where they are highly structured. Ability groups are not always formed on the basis of attainment. Behaviour is an important factor. This is recognised by pupils, as we saw earlier, and staff.

> We try our best – you have to be realistic, it's not always easy – in fact it's never easy because children don't fit into nice little categories. As well as academic issues, you also have to bear in mind things like social issues. It often happens that you've got a big group of boys at the bottom and that can make for behaviour problems so it's being aware of these things and trying to work out the best ways around them, I think. (Deputy head, school 3)

There is a danger that some groups within society may become disenfranchised because of ability grouping procedures. For instance, there is considerable recent evidence that African–Caribbean pupils are placed in lower-ability groups than their levels of attainment would indicate (Gillborn & Youdell 2000). While there is no recent UK evidence that structured ability grouping inhibits or promotes social mixing and cohesion, we do know that where education is divided on religious or ethnic grounds there is a tendency for social divisions to be exacerbated as there is no opportunity for the different groups to come to know each other better. We might therefore expect that social mixing and coherence would be promoted by mixed-ability classes.

Teachers' beliefs about ability grouping

The attitude of teachers towards ability grouping is crucial in relation to what goes on in the classroom (Barker Lunn 1970). Teachers who favour ability grouping tend to be 'knowledge' centred, with an emphasis on the acquisition of knowledge and the attainment of a set of academic standards. They are particularly interested in and concerned for the bright child, concentrate on traditional lessons, give more emphasis to literacy and numeracy, encourage competition and approve of selective examinations. Firm discipline is seen as important as the classroom atmosphere is formal. Teachers who favour mixed-ability grouping tend to be more child-centred, with a greater concern for the all-round development of each pupil. Teaching tends to stress self development, learning by discovery and practical experience. A more cooperative environment is encouraged, where pupils work in groups and help each other. There is also a more permissive classroom atmosphere. These teachers dislike streaming and selective examinations.

Preferences for teaching particular groups

Historically, where ability grouping structures have been in place, teachers have indicated preferences for teaching high-ability groups, in some cases competing against each other in order to be able to do so. Teachers of high-ability groups have tended to be more enthusiastic about their teaching and have perceived themselves as more successful, although this seems to have been mediated by the extent to which the pupils were engaged with their learning (Ireson & Hallam 2001). Pupils in lower-ability groups can be more difficult to interest and motivate which may undermine teachers' feelings of success. Teachers who consistently teach low-ability groups tend to become demoralised over a period of time. For instance:

> We had a lot of teachers who were dissatisfied because they always taught the lower streams. I looked at them and thought, you know, they'd lost their spark, so we needed to address that, and that's what we did. (Head teacher, school 4)

Pupils from high-ability groups tend to exhibit pro-social behaviour and it is this, rather than their academic achievement, that seems to shape teachers' behaviour towards them (Harlen & Malcolm 1997). Teachers interact with high-ability groups more frequently and positively than they do with low-ability groups, although in some schools there is evidence that teachers of low-stream pupils have viewed them positively. This may be particularly true in the current UK educational context, where some teachers have chosen to teach those with Special Educational Needs.

Differences in subjects

At secondary level, where teachers work within subject specialisms, the subject that they teach has a major impact on their attitudes towards structured ability grouping (Reid *et al.* 1982; Ireson & Hallam 2001). Where subjects are structured in such a way that learning builds on previous knowledge, for example in mathematics and modern foreign languages, teachers favour structured ability grouping, while the humanities and English are perceived as particularly suitable for mixed-ability teaching. Scientists occupy a middle position. Those subjects where mixed-ability teaching is perceived as problematic tend to require correct answers and a grasp of abstract concepts, those where mixed-ability teaching is seen as particularly appropriate are those where differentiation can occur through learning outcomes. While no systematic study of teachers' attitudes to ability grouping by subject has been undertaken at primary level, the evidence that mathematics is taught in ability groups, from the earliest years, suggests that there is a perception that it is appropriate for maths to be taught in this way. In contrast to the findings at secondary level, English is often ability grouped at primary level. This may reflect the greater emphasis on the acquisition of basic skills for young children.

Mathematics – the National Numeracy Strategy

Mathematics is the subject where there is the greatest level of ability grouping in the primary school. As we saw in Chapter 2, in the early years of schooling this tends to be within the class but in the later years, as national testing approaches, setting has become increasingly common. Guidance on the implementation of the National Numeracy Strategy suggests that in a typical 45–60 minute lesson, teachers should spend 5–10 minutes on oral work and mental calculation, 30–40 minutes on the main teaching activity and 10–15 minutes in a plenary with the whole class. The main teaching activity might be with the class as a whole, in which case teaching should be interactive, or it might involve work with groups, pairs or individuals. Group work should have a maximum of three levels of differentiatioń of an activity. During the first year of implementation of the numeracy hour, teachers were more likely to teach the whole class together during the main teaching activity (Ofsted 2000b).

The numeracy framework (DfEE 1999) does not advocate setting and stresses that any ability grouping arrangements implemented need to be flexible to allow easy transfer of pupils between sets. Schools are reminded that setting does not necessarily help to close the attainment gap across the year group and that children are quick to spot the significance of such ability groupings. Successful setting is seen to depend on very careful monitoring, close teamwork and cooperative planning among staff to make sure that expectations for all pupils are suitably high. The DfEE expects that as standards improve over time, the range of attainment in each year group should reduce, eliminating the need for setting. It is the quality of the teaching, not the adoption of structured groupings that is seen as important. The best numeracy performance is seen when teachers:

- devote a high proportion of lesson time to direct teaching of whole classes and groups, making judicious use of text books, work sheets and ICT resources to support teaching, not to replace it;
- ensure that differentiation is manageable and centred around work common to all the pupils in a class, with targeted, positive support to help those who have difficulties with maths to keep up with their peers.

Pupils with Special Educational Needs and the very able are expected to be taught with their own class. The assumption is that grouping will occur within the class (DfEE 1999). This will be dealt with in the next chapter.

The interim report on the National Numeracy Strategy (2000a) showed that around 20 per cent of schools had adopted setting for maths. Teachers in setted classes reported that it was easier to teach more precisely because of the narrower range of attainment. The quality of the teaching of the setted lessons as judged by inspectors was virtually the same as that of the non-setted lessons, although teaching of the top sets was better than that of the lower sets. Ofsted suggests that schools need to give particular thought to the deployment of teachers for setted lessons, especially to the likely impact of the more skilled teachers of maths on the attainment in a year group and the effect this could have on the proportion of pupils achieving level 4 by the age of 11. Despite the limitations of setting, at the end of the first year of the implementation of the numeracy strategy it had increased. Over a quarter of the schools visited were setting for maths, mainly in years 5 and 6 (Ofsted 2000b). The most experienced maths teachers were often deployed with year 5 or year 6 classes. It was this that contributed most to the high proportion of good teaching in years 5 and 6, not the setting itself.

Ofsted views the integration of SEN pupils into the numeracy hour as beneficial, although alternative strategies include withdrawing pupils or providing help through support teachers. Booster classes, which tend to concentrate on pupils who are borderline to achieve level 4, are welcomed by schools. Run within, before or after school, they are seen as particularly beneficial for schools with cross-age classes (Ofsted 2000b).

Overall, current guidance from the DfEE and Ofsted does not support setting for numeracy. It is considered that the structure of the numeracy hour itself, where within-class grouping is integral and flexible groups are used, is sufficient to ensure the appropriate balance of differentiation and integration and maximum progress for all pupils.

English – the National Literacy Strategy

As we saw in Chapter 2, the subject where primary school pupils were most likely to be grouped by ability after mathematics was English. This contrasts with secondary school, where English is usually taught in mixed-ability classes. The difference is almost certainly rooted in the greater emphasis on basic skills at primary level. The guidance for the literacy hour indicates that for approximately 40 minutes all the children in the class should be taught together. During the remaining 20 minutes, teachers should work with groups of pupils on guided reading and writing, while the remainder of the class complete independent work (DfEE 1998). Setting is not a recommended option and should only occur in specific circumstances. Schools have interpreted the guidance in different ways depending on their previous practice, perceptions of the range of attainment within the class, and available resources.

The intention of the literacy hour has been to shift the balance of teaching from individualised work, especially in the teaching of reading, towards more whole-class and group teaching. The group and independent work sessions are to enable the teacher to teach at least one ability group per day for a sustained period through guided reading or writing. This time is also to enable other pupils to work independently – individually, in pairs or in groups without requesting the assistance of the teacher. Although ability grouping within the class is specified, setting is only considered to be justified in some circumstances, for instance, in classes with more than two year groups or where reception children are taught with years 1 and 2. In this case, four options are suggested:

- reducing the amount of whole-class time to allow for more group time;
- increasing the group time while retaining the whole-class teaching time (i.e. extending the hour);
- making use of an additional adult to provide simultaneous teaching or support; and
- setting across a number of classes, although this should not be allowed to lower expectations.

The guidance suggests that schools should be flexible in adopting these different procedures. The curriculum has been planned so that it can be adopted as a two-year rolling programme (often adopted with mixed-age classes) with only minor adjustments being necessary. Schools are advised to avoid having classes split across key stages, wherever possible, or including children from the same year group in two different-age classes. An alternative is that teachers divide the class teaching times between two main groups, to focus on older and younger pupils using an additional adult, or re-group through setting or co-operative teaching. Withdrawing children from the literacy hour should only occur in response to particular or severe needs. The DfEE suggests that most pupils with English as an Additional Language should be fully included.

As in numeracy, schools have been funded to provide booster classes. These enable additional support to be given to pupils on the borderline between levels 3 and 4, usually through the creation of an additional teaching group run within, before or after school. The Additional

Literacy Support (ALS) initiative was also introduced in 1999 to provide help for lower-attaining pupils in years 3 and 4.

As in maths, setting is not advocated as part of the literacy strategy. The activities designated to be undertaken within the literacy hour are seen to provide appropriate within-class differentiation while maintaining opportunities for the less able to be stretched and provided with high-quality models of good work.

Parental concerns

The market economy that now exists in education has increased the pressure on schools to take account of the views of parents in relation to ability grouping. Although parents tend to believe that some form of structured ability grouping is best, there are tensions when their own children are not placed in the top group or when they are being moved down a group. For example:

> It's a shame that the parents can't be more understanding! They'd like a top set of 90 children, and at the end of the day you're playing a numbers game and it's very hard getting over to the parents the idea that whatever set they're in they're working flat out. (Head teacher, school 4)

How schools can manage the process of moving pupils between groups will be considered fully in Chapter 6.

Parents' expectations are also shaped on the basis of their child's group classification. Barker Lunn (1970) surveyed parents' attitudes and revealed that at primary level the classification of pupils was interpreted by parents as an indication of their child's future. Where schools did not stream, the links between the ability of the child and parental aspirations were less close.

When are systems of structured ability grouping likely to be beneficial?

Our current knowledge about learning demonstrates that the speed and ease with which individuals learn depends on the extent of their prior knowledge and their current level of expertise. Both may vary in relation to different subject domains. For this reason there can be very little justification for the adoption of streaming, which assumes a single unitary intelligence that is exhibited in similar performance across different subjects. The fact that only two per cent of schools appear to be adopting streaming suggests that this is now well accepted. Setting overcomes this problem by taking account of differences in attainment across subject domains. It has a number of strengths:

- Pupils and teachers agree that it enables work to be more closely matched to pupil needs;
- Teachers find it easier to plan and teach when the range of prior attainment in the class is restricted;
- Teachers find classroom management easier;
- It encourages the adoption of whole-class teaching;
- The expertise of the best qualified teachers can be used to best effect in teaching the more able pupils.

It also has weaknesses:

- Pupils may be set work at an inappropriate level;
- Teachers may insufficiently differentiate work within the set;
- The pace of work in high sets can be stressful and may be at the expense of deep understanding;
- Low attainers are often insufficiently challenged and given work that is too easy;
- Low attainers lack higher-attaining role models and examples of high-quality work;
- The best teachers are often allocated to teach the higher sets leaving the lower sets with teachers with lower levels of expertise;
- Time can be wasted as pupils move to different sets;
- Where setting occurs in several subjects, class teachers report lacking overall knowledge of pupil progress;
- Pupil movement between groups is usually limited, leading to rigidity;
- Placement of pupils in ability groups is not always based on attainment, other factors such as behaviour are often important;
- Setting can lead to stigmatisation of those in the lowest sets and teasing of those in the highest sets.

As can be seen in the guidance provided for the numeracy and literacy strategies, setting is beneficial when the range of attainment in a particular group of pupils is so wide that teaching them together becomes impossible. In small schools where there are cross-age classes spanning more than two year groups this may be particularly relevant. In most other cases within-class ability grouping can be as effective as setting and offers the advantage of greater flexibility.

Minimising the possible negative effects of setting

If teachers believe that the range of attainment in a class is so great that some form of setting is necessary, attempts can be made to minimise the negative effects. In practice this means that:

- Children should remain in mixed-ability classes for the greater part of the time. Their main point of identification should be with a mixed-ability class;
- Structured ability grouping should be adopted only where teaching and learning in the subject domain depend on pupils having shared prior knowledge and levels of attainment;
- Procedures for assigning pupils to sets should be based on attainment in that particular subject, not general achievement or other factors, for example behaviour;
- Progress should be assessed frequently followed by reassignment to different groups where appropriate;
- Where necessary 'bridging' groups should be set up to enable pupils to cover work needed for moving to a higher group;
- Within groups, teachers must vary their pace and level of instruction to correspond to students' needs, adopting a range of methods and resources;
- Some differentiation of work should occur within the class;
- High-status teachers should be allocated to teach across the sets;
- Teachers should have high expectations of pupils in the lower sets;
- Pupils should not be denied access to the curriculum because of their group placement;
- The school should provide those pupils who are less academically able with opportunities to excel in other areas;
- The school should demonstrate that it values all of its pupils.

If setting is adopted within this framework the disadvantages will be minimised.

Conclusion

The particular benefit of setting is that it allows work to be set at an appropriate level for the pupil and makes the management of learning easier for the teacher. If the drawbacks can be minimised as outlined above then it may be an effective grouping practice, although at primary level much can be achieved by within-class ability grouping. The danger for schools is the development of an ethos that stresses academic achievement to the exclusion of all else; an environment where high ability is reified leaving the majority of pupils feeling unvalued with a subsequent loss to their self-esteem, confidence and academic attainment.

Chapter summary: streaming and setting

Structured ability grouping:

- does not, of itself, raise standards;
- can have negative effects on the personal development of some children;
- where adopted universally, can lead to a lack of social cohesion.

In school, adopting structured ability groupings:

- enables teachers to more easily differentiate the curriculum and match work to pupil needs;
- encourages whole-class teaching;
- leads to different pedagogical practices for pupils in different streams or sets;
- can lead to too low expectations of those in the lower sets or streams;
- legitimises the differential treatment of pupils of different abilities;
- can lead to the stigmatisation and teasing of pupils at either end of the attainment range.

Setting is not recommended in the national literacy and numeracy strategies.

Parents tend to support the principles of ability grouping but often experience difficulty in coming to terms with their offspring's group placement.

Further reading

Hallam, S. (2002) *Ability grouping in schools: a literature review.* London: Institute of Education, University of London.

Ireson, J. & Hallam, S. (2001) *Ability grouping in education.* London: Sage.

Chapter 5

Mixed-ability and within-class groupings

Introduction

The shift in educational values in the 1960s towards equal opportunities and a more child-centred approach led to a decline in streaming and an increase in mixed-ability classes (Lee & Croll 1995). Advocated by the Plowden Report, this trend continued through the 1970s in the belief that mixed-ability classes would provide all pupils with equal access to a common curriculum and would promote the matching of individual learning programmes to the needs of individual pupils (DES 1978). This required the teacher to move away from whole-class teaching towards providing individual work tailored to the needs of each child (Gregory 1986). The Plowden Report recognised that it would be difficult to translate this ideal into practice and group work within the class was seen as a means of making it possible. As we shall see in this chapter, in most classrooms the ideal was never attained and groups have tended to be used as a means of managing the class rather than as a vehicle for teaching and learning. In this chapter we will consider:

- the advantages of mixed-ability classes;
- the rationale for group work in the primary classroom;
- classroom layout;
- group size;
- whole-class mixed-ability teaching;
- within-class groupings – ability and mixed-ability;
- working in pairs;
- individualised learning programmes;
- vertical grouping;
- special activity groups;
- teacher skills; and
- planning.

Advantages of mixed-ability classes

The key advantage of mixed-ability classes is the flexibility that they offer the teacher in being able to provide a range of individual, group and whole-class learning opportunities for pupils where group composition can be changed easily and with minimum disruption. In addition mixed-ability classes can:

- provide a means of ensuring that all pupils have equal opportunities;
- encourage cooperative behaviour and social integration;
- provide positive role models for less able pupils;
- promote good relations between pupils;
- enhance pupil–teacher interactions;
- reduce some of the competition engendered by structured grouping;
- allow pupils to work at their own pace;
- force teachers to acknowledge that the pupils in their class are not a homogeneous group; and
- encourage teachers to identify pupil needs and match learning tasks to them.

Although in the past, teachers have tended to use groups as a means of managing the classroom, they can be used as a means to focus teaching and promote learning.

The rationale for group work in the primary classroom

Group work was introduced into the primary classroom as a way of providing a more individualised programme of work for each pupil. Teaching small groups was seen as a compromise between the ideal of individualised teaching and the impracticalities of this within the state education system. As the Plowden Report acknowledged, 'Only seven or eight minutes a day would be available for each child, if all teaching were individual' (DES 1967: 274). Despite this, teachers are more likely to engage with pupils as individuals than in group or whole-class activities (Galton *et al.* 1980; Croll & Moses 1988; Mortimore *et al.* 1988; Pollard *et al.* 1994). The extent of individual interactions as reported in research has ranged from 50 to 72 per cent; whole-class interactions from 16 to 32 per cent and group interactions from 9 to

19 per cent. Recently, there has been an increase in whole-class inter-actions and a decrease in individual interactions, but typically teachers have not worked with pupils in groups. For each pupil, the time spent in interaction with the teacher is relatively small. On average pupils spend less than a sixth of their time in interaction with their teacher and much of this is as part of whole-class teaching sessions. Children spend about one minute in every hour in one-to-one interaction with the teacher and the same proportion of time in a group with which the teacher is interacting (Croll 1996).

If teachers spend relatively little time interacting with pupils does this have an impact on pupil learning? The evidence suggests that it does. There is a significant positive relationship between the amount of time the teacher spends interacting with the class and progress in a wide range of areas (Mortimore et al. 1988). Students achieve more in classes where they spend most of their time being taught or supervised by their teachers rather than working on their own (Brophy & Good 1986).

Underlying the relationship between the extent of pupil–teacher interaction and progress may be the amount of time that pupils spend on task. Time on task has been shown to be a predictor of academic attainment (Brophy & Good 1986). In addition, when pupils are not on task they may misbehave and disrupt the work of others. Whole-class teaching is positively associated with time on task and pupil engagement with their work (Galton et al. 1980; Pollard et al. 1994). Where teachers spend more time in whole-class teaching, pupils are more on task when undertaking individual work (Croll & Moses 1988).

It is important to maximise the extent of teacher–pupil interaction and the amount of time that pupils spend actively engaged with their work. How can these aims be achieved? In *Curriculum organisation and classroom practice in primary schools*, Alexander et al. (1992) suggest that teachers must find an appropriate balance between whole-class, group and individual work. As we saw in Chapter 4, the literacy and numeracy strategies set out activities that attempt to achieve such a balance. We will now explore how teachers might plan other activities to maximise pupil engagement with learning and teacher–pupil interaction.

Classroom layout

The layout of the classroom is an important determinant of the way that teachers are able to organise groups. Until the 1960s most classrooms in the UK were set out in rows. There was a move to group seating after the Plowden Report (DES 1967) and this is now normal practice in most primary classrooms (Hastings *et al.* 1996). On-task behaviour increases and rates of disruption are lower when pupils are seated in rows rather than around tables in groups (see Hastings *et al.* 1996 for a review of research). Children spend a markedly greater proportion of their time actively engaged with individual work when seated in rows. The size of the difference is substantial. Increases in time on task between the two seating arrangements range from 16 per cent to 124 per cent across a range of studies (Hastings *et al.* 1996). Analysis of the behaviour of individual children has demonstrated that those children normally least on task benefit most from the changed seating arrangements (Wheldall *et al.* 1981; Hastings & Schwieso 1995).

An increasingly popular seating arrangement that gives the teacher easy access to individuals and retains the advantages of rows is a U shape. This can be used for whole-class teaching, individual and paired work. Tables on wheels can be easily moved from this arrangement to an arrangement more conducive to group work when necessary. For literacy and numeracy this should be no more than 4 ability groups to enable teachers to spend a substantial amount of time teaching each group. Although children will generally be in different groups for literacy and numeracy the table arrangements can be the same. The children will merely sit at different tables.

Groups set up for literacy and numeracy will be too large for collaborative group work. A further arrangement will therefore be needed to enable smaller mixed-ability groups to work on other curricular tasks (see Table 5.1). Using the U shape as the normal classroom arrangement, children can very quickly learn to move tables to either of the other arrangements as appropriate. A strength of this arrangement is that the normal seating arrangement (the U shape) is mixed-ability and does not categorise children as being of a particular ability in relation to either literacy or numeracy.

Table 5.1 Room arrangements for grouping activities

Room arrangement	Type of activity
U shaped arrangement	Whole-class teaching, individual work, paired work
Tables arranged for 3 or 4 large groups	Teaching and ability-grouped work in the numeracy and literacy hours
Tables arranged for groups of up to 6 pupils	Mixed-ability groups for collaborative work in other curriculum areas

Group size

The size of groups can be thought of as on a continuum ranging from a single individual to very large groups. The optimal size of groups varies depending on the activity to be undertaken. If groups are large, there is less likelihood that everyone will participate (Nasati & Clements 1991; Jaques 2000). In larger groups there can also be a diffusion of responsibility where group members believe it is not their responsibility to ensure that a task is completed (Webb 1989). In the primary school classroom, group size can vary from the whole class, through large ability groups for teaching purposes, smaller groups of four to six for collaborative work, and pairs to the individual. Groups of three are the most likely to bring out power disparities between pupils (two siding against one) unless the teacher deliberately structures tasks to avoid this, e.g. working with computers where one child operates the computer and the other two discuss problems, or problem solving where one high-attaining pupil works with two low-attaining pupils (see Kutnick 1994 for details). As a general rule triads are to be avoided.

Whole-class mixed-ability teaching

Following the Plowden Report (1967), there was criticism of whole-class teaching because instruction tended to be targeted at an 'imaginary average' child even though the range of abilities indicated that differentiation was necessary (HMI 1978; Wragg 1984; Hacker & Rowe 1993). Recently, it has been recognised that whole-class mixed-ability teaching can have positive educational effects. It is an efficient means of transmitting information to a large number of children simultaneously providing order, control, purpose and concentration (Alexander *et al*. 1992). It has been adopted as a key element in the national literacy and numeracy strategies with specific guidance as to how the sessions should be taught so that all pupils are engaged and actively participating.

Within-class groupings

While within-class groupings can take many forms, the range of groupings normally implemented is rather limited. Several different kinds of group work have been identified: joint group work, where pupils engage in specific tasks that contribute to an overall theme;

seated group work, where children sit together but work individually, albeit undertaking the same work; and cooperative group work, where ideas are pooled as part of a joint piece of work (Galton *et al.* 1980). Observation of classes has revealed that 80 per cent of group work is seated group work (Galton *et al.* 1980; Galton *et al.* 1987). Joint group work is found in most classrooms (Galton 1981) and is generally used in art, craft and general studies but not in relation to basic skills. There is little collaborative work. While within-class grouping of various types has been adopted in primary schools in the UK over a number of years (Harlen & Malcolm 1997), it has usually been on a rather informal basis (Hallam & Toutounji 1996a). Group composition has tended to be based on decisions about classroom management and much group work has been described as limited and impoverished, time being spent undertaking trivial tasks (HMI 1978, 1979; Reid *et al.* 1982). The cognitive demands made on students tend to be low, as is the quality of the verbal interactions between pupils (Sands & Kerry 1982; Kerry & Sands 1984). Few group tasks make sufficient cognitive demands on the more able and in many cases do not stretch average pupils.

Although group work has not been implemented regularly or systematically in the UK, it can have positive academic and social effects for all pupils (Creemers 1994). The need for a greater emphasis on group work within the classroom has been stressed frequently. This may be in ability groups to assist in the acquisition of basic skills through increasing interaction between teachers and pupils (DES 1978; Barker Lunn 1984; Mortimore *et al.* 1988) or in mixed-ability groups to undertake particular tasks. Within-class grouping provides teachers with the opportunity to meet the needs of pupils of different abilities while reducing the problems inherent in managing individualised learning. Pupils can support each other, motivation can be increased and pressure on the teacher may be reduced. Pupils also have the opportunity to develop their social and communication skills. For some, it can provide an informal context where they are less inhibited about expressing themselves. This is well articulated by one teacher:

> I think it's far more informal when they're in groups as opposed to whole class. It's far more open and the children don't feel as though they're on display as much, especially the child that is particularly reticent to speak out loud in a whole class situation – you find that suddenly in a group situation, they come alive and it's nice to hear their voice and their opinions being aired. I think that definitely when they're grouped, you're more informal and there's more

variety in your questioning because you've got so many different points of view than you would have in a whole-class situation where there is a tendency for the more able to dominate. (Key Stage 2 teacher, school 4)

Given the reported benefits of within-class groupings we will now examine how they can be best implemented and for what purposes.

Within-class ability groupings

Research on collaborative group work has indicated that it is more effective when it is carried out in mixed-ability groups. However, there may be circumstances where teachers wish to group pupils within the class by ability for instructional purposes and the setting of work. The main advantage of adopting ability grouping structures within as opposed to between classes is their flexibility. Pupils can be moved between groups easily and teachers can restructure groupings regularly based on their knowledge of pupil progress, levels of achievement, behaviour and rates of work.

Teachers have often seated pupils by ability but the work undertaken has often been individual. Able pupils have sometimes acted as teacher's aides to help the slower learners. Overall, however, group work has tended to be used as an organisational device (Galton *et al.* 1980).

The optimum size of within-class ability groups depends on their purpose. For instructional purposes, the DfEE, in relation to the numeracy and literacy strategies, advises that there should be few groups, three or four in each class. This is to enable the teacher to spend a substantial amount of time instructing each group. If pupils are to work without the assistance of the teacher, within-class ability grouping is most effective when it occurs with groups of four pupils (Lou *et al.* 1996). Groupings of such small numbers will inevitably reduce the amount of time that a teacher can spend with any particular group. Such groups are most productive when they work together over a number of weeks (Lou *et al.* 1996).

In the case study schools, teachers working with ability groups within their class adjusted their teaching in much the same way as those teachers working with sets of different levels. For example:

It depends on the subject really. For maths, when they're usually in ability groups, I might tend to use more practical activities to explain things, and move at a slower pace with lots of reinforcement and revision for the less able groups. When they're in mixed-ability groups, it really depends on what they're doing – it's hard to be specific. I suppose I use more visual materials with the less able, but there again, I generally use them with the whole class and just adjust my expectations and demands according to the child's ability. (Key Stage 2 teacher, school 6)

The level at which you pitch things is different. For the higher-ability groups, you can pitch things so much higher. They come out with their own ideas so much quicker than the lower groups. I think that in terms of reactive teaching, you could go along with a higher-ability group and take them wherever you wanted, and so much faster. With the lower-ability group, things have to be pitched far more at their needs and the group work obviously is a really important factor to make sure that their needs are catered for. (Key Stage 2 teacher, school 6)

Grouping pupils by ability is an integral part of the literacy and numeracy strategies.

The National Literacy Strategy

The evaluation of the implementation of the National Literacy Strategy at the end of the second year (Ofsted 2000) indicated that successful operation of the ability group work included controlled differentiation of tasks so that as few different activities as possible were being undertaken. This enabled the teacher to maintain the focus of all the work on the same teaching objectives. A high proportion of the most successful independent work took place when all the pupils were engaged in tasks relating to a common starting point with similar objectives (Ofsted 2000).

Another feature is the teacher being able to work uninterrupted with one of the groups:

In the literacy hour you might introduce a topic to one group, then they can work on that and then you can spend your time with another group so that you sort of have to structure your work so that you know that when you have to home in on one group, then the other groups are doing things that they can cope with without you. Also, I think that it's down to the sort of planning in the beginning and the way that you teach the children and when you can be disrupted if you like, and when you can't be. They tend to understand that I think – if you're working as a group, and if I'm actually sitting down with a group of children around me then I don't really want to be disturbed unless it's really, really important. They can ask an assistant or something like this. I think that it does get easier the older the children are and the more used to the routine they are. (Key Stage 2 teacher, school 3)

The National Numeracy Strategy

The key thrust of the National Numeracy Strategy is to enable teachers to devote a high proportion of lesson time to the direct teaching of whole classes and groups. Organising pupils as a 'whole' class for a significant proportion of the time helps to maximise their contact with the teacher so that every child benefits from the teaching and interaction for sustained periods. Text books, work sheets and ICT resources should be used to support teaching but not as a substitute for it. Differentiation should be manageable and centred around work common to all the pupils in a class, with targeted positive support to help those who have difficulties with maths to keep up with their peers (DfEE 1999). Where differentiation is organised through group activities it should not exceed three levels. In most classes this will mean that ability groups will be large, a third of the class. This is to ensure that the teacher's attention is not divided between too many groups.

The DfEE suggests that good teaching in the numeracy hour requires the balancing of different elements including:

- directing;
- instructing;
- demonstrating;
- explaining and illustrating;
- questioning and discussing;
- consolidating;
- evaluating pupils' responses; and
- summarising.

A typical numeracy lesson consists of whole-class oral work and mental calculation; the main teaching activity which can include work as a whole class, in groups, in pairs or as individuals; followed by a plenary to conclude where misconceptions are corrected, progress is identified, key facts are summarised, links are made with other work, next steps are discussed and homework may be set.

Within-class mixed-ability groupings

Groups working together without the teacher work best when they are mixed-ability and include the most and least able. High-ability pupils are crucial for effective group functioning but they also benefit as the process of working in groups serves to enhance their own skills (Bennett & Cass 1989; Swing & Peterson 1982; Webb 1991). Where classes are cross-age, groups should reflect this with a mixture of younger and older pupils. They should also reflect the ethnic mix of the class and have a gender balance (Slavin 1990). Allocating pupils to groups in this way can promote social mixing and break down stereotypical views of other pupils.

Allocation of pupils to mixed-ability groups is often made on an *ad hoc* basis. Groups are typically between four and six pupils and there is considerable variability regarding how they are formed. Some teachers assign pupils to groups, some allow pupils to choose and others operate some form of negotiation (Hastings *et al.* 1996). Gender appears to be an important organisational device used by teachers (Pollard *et al.* 1994; Wragg 1993). Mixed-gender groups can increase the amount of time the group spends on task (Wheldall & Olds 1987). As we saw in Chapter 3, pupils are aware that manipulating gender can improve behaviour and task focus. When allowed to choose where to sit, pupils tend to choose same gender groups (Galton *et al.* 1980), and as we saw earlier often resent having to be in mixed-gender groups, particularly when the balance is unequal and they are isolated within a group of the opposite gender.

A distinction is usually made between cooperative and collaborative group work. In cooperative group work each pupil has a separate but related task and there is a joint outcome to which each pupil contributes a separate element. In collaborative work all pupils share the same task and there is one shared learning outcome, for instance, the outcome of a discussion (Bennett & Dunne 1989; Galton & Williamson 1992). In practice, there is often not a clear distinction between these different types of group work.

Cooperative and collaborative groupings

Cooperative and collaborative group work has not been implemented extensively in primary classrooms in the UK. While pupils have often been seated in groups they have tended to work on individual tasks. Where group work has been undertaken it has tended to be related to topic work, problem solving, data collection, creative tasks and where the multiple perspectives of group members can elaborate an issue. In the USA group work has been adopted in a more systematic way.

An early approach was known as 'Jigsaw' (Aronson 1978). Here, each member of the group is provided with only one section of the material that is to be learned. Each member studies their section with members of an expert group who are all studying the same section. They then return to their own group and teach the section to the others. All members of the group are then tested on all parts of the task. Groups are formed of five to six pupils and are mixed in ability.

An alternative approach provides pupils with broader and more diverse learning experiences (Johnson & Johnson 1975). The process consists of six stages. Pupils identify sub-topics within an area identified by the teacher and organise themselves into groups of three to six children. The group plans the task, which is usually some form of problem solving, determines the goal and how it is to be studied. The information is collected, analysed and evaluated before a final report, event or summary is prepared. This is then presented to the class, who evaluate the work. This mirrors the process most frequently adopted in UK schools when group work is undertaken.

Recent formulations of cooperative group work have refined earlier ideas. All the methods have in common that pupils work together to learn and are responsible for one another's learning as well as their own. There are three fundamental principles: rewards are given to teams; each individual is accountable for their own contribution; each team member must have an equal opportunity to be successful. For example, in Student Teams–Achievement Divisions (STAD) (Slavin 1983) pupils are assigned to four member learning teams mixed in prior levels of knowledge, gender and ethnicity. The teacher presents the material to be learned. The pupils then work in teams to ensure that they have all mastered the lesson. Pupils are then tested on the material to be learned. At this point they must work independently. Scores are compared to past team averages and points are awarded on the degree to which past performance is matched or exceeded. The points are summed to derive team scores and from this teams meeting certain criteria may earn further rewards. The whole process is undertaken over a number of lessons. Such techniques have been adopted with learners of all ages, from age seven to college entrance. They are most appropriate for areas with well-defined learning objectives. A variant replaces the tests with competitions, which provides an added incentive for the children.

Another alternative is called Team Assisted Individualisation (Slavin 1983). This combines cooperative learning with individualised instruction and was designed to be used in maths lessons. The teams are set up with four members of different prior knowledge and ability. The pupils enter an individualised sequence of work based on a test of their prior knowledge of that topic. They then proceed to work at their own pace. Team members check each other's work and help each other with problems. Final unit tests are taken without help and are marked by pupil monitors. Each week the teacher totals the units acquired by each team. Rewards are then given for team performance. The teacher's time in class is spent on explaining new topics to small groups of children drawn from the various teams who are working on the same topic or level, so although the teams are mixed-ability, the teacher works with pupils of the same ability.

If the procedures are undertaken appropriately cooperative grouping can be a very effective way of supporting academic learning and can also have positive social effects (Slavin 1990). Learning outcomes vary according to the quality of the method used and how well it is implemented. Two things are important for success: group goals and individual accountability. When these are both present, the results are consistently positive. In addition, cooperative learning rarely has negative effects and does not hold back able pupils. Where cooperative learning is adopted children express greater liking for their classmates. It promotes ethnic mixing and inter-ability friendships and improves attitudes to school. It also increases self-esteem, has positive effects on achievement for all children, and improves the integration of children with Special Educational Needs (Slavin 1990). Although there has been some criticism of this approach (Bennett 1985), its implementation in Holland, where there are certain cultural similarities with the United Kingdom (Roeders 1989), has shown positive academic and social outcomes. Where it is unsuccessful it is often because the procedures have been inappropriately applied, teachers failing to carry out the necessary testing, recording of progress and feedback procedures. In the USA, teachers have found the methods easy to use and pupils seem to like them. They provide an appropriate means of structuring and managing within-class groups. Such groupings provide pupils with structured opportunities to learn from each other while being able to demonstrate a degree of independence from the teacher. At all levels where they have been deployed they have been demonstrated to be effective (Creemers 1994; Cohen 1994).

Group processes

The kinds of interactions that occur between pupils when they are working on particular tasks in groups and the effects of particular types of group work have been identified. Taken together the evidence suggests that:

- When pupils work in groups on specific tasks self-esteem and motivation can be enhanced (Galton & Williamson 1992; Slavin 1990);
- Teachers need to encourage groups to work independently and rarely intervene so that decisions are reached by the group (Harwood 1989; Cohen 1994; Slavin 1990);
- Group work is valuable for the development of exploratory talk (Barnes et al. 1969; Barnes & Todd 1977; Tough 1977);
- Success in group tasks depends on pupils' ability to raise questions, to listen attentively to each other and to manage disputes whenever they arise (Tann 1981);
- Group processes and performance differ depending on the nature of the task (Tann 1981; Biott 1987; Bennett & Dunne 1989; Cohen 1994);
- Levels of interaction are higher when the task is practical (Bennett 1985);
- When the task involves discussion of abstract ideas the level of interaction may be low but of a high quality. Teachers should not be discouraged by this (Dunne & Bennett 1990; Galton & Williamson 1992);
- Problem-solving tasks with a clear measurable outcome tend to generate a higher level of collaboration than open-ended tasks (Crozier & Kleinberg 1987);
- Pupils need to be taught how to collaborate. This involves the teacher setting clear goals and giving immediate feedback on progress through discussion (Biott 1987; Webb 1983, 1985; Burden et al. 1988; Glaye 1986).

Discussions within groups that lead to positive task achievement follow a developmental pattern (Webb 1989). Pupils 'scaffold' the problem for others, provide reciprocal teaching, resolve conflicts and model various processes of understanding. They must be able to ask for and receive help from other group members and develop skills of explanation and elaboration. Crucial is sensitivity to the needs of others. To develop these skills pupils need guidance from the teacher on how to build relationships and cohesiveness among the group and how to assist successful task completion. Table 5.2 sets out actions that will support group development and cohesiveness. Before introducing group work, teachers may find it useful to lead the whole class in developing simple rules of conduct and making it clear to pupils that they are expected to work cooperatively. Ideally, guidance should be implemented at whole-school level so all the pupils have a shared understanding of what is acceptable behaviour within the group context.

Table 5.2 Group building and maintenance skills

> Encouraging – being friendly, warm, responsive to others, praising others and their ideas, agreeing with and accepting the contributions of others;
>
> Mediating – harmonising, conciliating differences in points of view, making compromises;
>
> Gatekeeping – trying to make it possible for another group member to make a contribution when they are being ignored by others;
>
> Standard setting – expressing standards for the group to adopt including procedures, rules of conduct, ethical values;
>
> Following – going along with the group, accepting the ideas of others, serving as an audience during group discussion, being a good listener;
>
> Relieving tension – diverting attention away from unpleasant disagreements by making jokes, changing the direction of discussion.
>
> (Derived from Jaques 2000)

Group work requires group members to function in relation to particular tasks. In many cases in the primary school these will require practical action but during the planning phase, other skills will be required. These include:

- Initiating – suggesting new ideas or a changed way of looking at the group problem or goal, proposing new activities;
- Information seeking – asking for relevant facts or information;
- Information giving – providing relevant facts or information or relating personal experience relevant to the group task;
- Opinion giving – stating a relevant belief or opinion about something the group is considering;
- Clarifying – probing for meaning and understanding, restating something the group is considering;

- Elaborating – building on a previous comment, enlarging on it, giving examples;
- Coordinating – showing or clarifying the relationships between various ideas, trying to pull ideas and suggestions together;
- Orienting – defining the progress of the discussion in terms of the group's goals, raising questions about the direction the discussion is taking;
- Testing – checking with the group to see if it is ready to make a decision or to take some action;
- Summarising – reviewing the content of past discussion.

(Derived from Jaques 2000)

It may also be useful for teachers to outline to their pupils the kinds of behaviour which will not contribute towards successful group work. Some examples are set out in Table 5.3.

Table 5.3 Examples of behaviour likely to disrupt group work

Blocking – interfering with the progress of the group by going off at a tangent;

Aggressing – criticising or blaming others, showing hostility towards the group or some individual, attacking the motives of others, deliberately deflating the ego of others;

Seeking recognition – attempting to call attention to oneself by excessive talking, extreme ideas, boasting or over-activity;

Special pleading – introducing or supporting ideas related to one's own pet ideas or concerns;

Withdrawing – acting indifferent or passive, resorting to excessive formality, doodling, whispering to others;

Dominating – trying to assert authority in manipulating the group by pulling rank, giving directions, interrupting others' contributions.

(Derived from Jaques 2000)

Working in pairs

Paired work is particularly suited for well-defined tasks which can be undertaken in a relatively short time. It can take the form of peer tutoring, where one child is seen as more expert than the other and takes on a teaching role, or as an exchange between equals. It provides opportunities for discussion, explanation and elaboration in a cooperative and unthreatening way and has the advantage that it does not usually require pupils to move from their current seats. A wide range of tasks can be tackled and paired work is specified as being a useful element of the numeracy hour.

Individualised learning programmes

Despite the emphasis in the Plowden Report on the need to develop individualised learning programmes for pupils, few teachers have adopted this strategy (Kerry & Sands 1984). The exception has been where pupils have used work cards, specific text books, often in maths, or where schools have adopted particular reading schemes. In the USA, systems of individualised instruction have been developed that do operate successfully, particularly with older students. The Personalised System of Instruction (PSI), an individualised mastery learning programme, has proved effective for older students in a range of environments. Successful individualised programmes are based on instruction tailored to the assessed abilities of each student. Students work at their own pace, receive periodic reports on their mastery and plan and evaluate their own learning. Alternative materials and activities are provided to assist them. Where these criteria are satisfied, individualised programmes have been shown to be more effective than whole-class instruction in relation to academic and personal learning outcomes (Waxman et al. 1985). Learning programmes based on such rigid learning objectives have not proved popular in the UK, although an individualised programme known as 'school based flexible learning' has shown considerable promise in geography teaching at secondary level (Hughes 1993).

Vertical grouping

As we saw in Chapter 2, a large proportion of primary schools, of necessity, have to adopt vertical grouping structures – that is putting children in classes that include more than one year group. Vertical grouping has been adopted as a system of choice by some schools because of the social and family-like structure of classes where pupils, at least one year apart in age, are taught by the same teacher together for several years. The purported benefits of vertical grouping are similar to those made for mixed-ability teaching (Veenman 1995):

- Students have the opportunity to form relationships with a wider variety of children;
- Teaching such a wide diversity of students demands that teaching is individualised;
- The complex and changing social environment in such classes encourages the development of a balanced personality;
- The self-concepts of the less able older children are enhanced when they are asked to help younger students;
- The student stays with the same teacher for more than one year, allowing closer and more secure relationships to develop;
- Fewer anxieties about learning develop because the atmosphere is conducive to academic and social growth;
- Younger students can benefit from the opportunity to observe, emulate and imitate a wide range of behaviours exhibited by older students;
- Older students have the opportunity to take responsibility for younger students;
- Vertical grouping promotes cooperation and other forms of pro-social behaviours, minimises competition and the need for discipline;
- The use of different learning materials provides opportunities for younger students to benefit from exposure to more advanced curricula while providing older students with the opportunity to benefit from reviewing earlier work;
- Students at different levels of cognitive development can provide intellectual stimulation for each other;
- Vertical grouping enables a relaxation of the rigid curriculum with its age-graded expectations which are not appropriate for all pupils.

Reviews of the effects of vertical grouping (Pratt 1986; Miller 1990; Veenman 1995) have concluded that there are no significant differences between cross-age and single-age groupings on pupils' academic achievement or social and personal development. However, teachers tend to hold negative attitudes about teaching cross-age classes. They find that it increases their work load, that the management of the class is more difficult because they perceive that they are trying to teach more than one class simultaneously, there is less opportunity for oral instruction because teaching one group may disrupt the other, there are more interruptions in the learning process, pupils receive less individual attention and it is harder for pupils to concentrate on their work. Teachers also comment that in general they do not receive training for vertical grouping (Veenman 1995). However, cross-age or vertical grouping practices have been adopted in the US targeted at particular areas of learning, e.g. literacy. This can be successful (Gutierrez & Slavin 1992). Some schools in the UK have successfully adopted cross-age setting to promote increased attainment in maths and literacy. For example:

> I inherited a very rigid junior–infant gap, with the children in the infant department sat in year groups for the whole of the time they were infants and similarly in the juniors. The only time that there was flexibility in the groupings was for art and PE and things like that, but for all the academic subjects they were sat at their table groups, in their year group, and they worked from specific pages in their work books whether it be phonics or English or whatever. I changed all that – my rationale being that children develop at different times and in different ways, particularly in the younger end, for example the boys not developing as quickly as the girls. So, I've tried to cater for that by allowing for as much flexibility in the groupings as possible and they'll move up and down over the year with discussion with the teachers involved. (Head teacher, school 5)

Schools that have cross-age classes have even greater flexibility in setting up groupings than those with same-age groupings. Pupils can be grouped according to age, ability and in mixed-ability groups depending on the nature of the task and their needs.

Special activity groups

Withdrawing children from classes has traditionally been used in the UK to provide additional support for children experiencing difficulties in specific areas, often literacy. However, the principle of providing 'special activities' can be applied to groups formed across or within year groups or within classes for a very wide range of purposes.

Activity groups can be set up to satisfy particular short term needs for particular groups of pupils, for example intensive literacy or numeracy 'booster' groups. Time might be allocated each week within the time-table to offer a range of special activities, for example, extension or catch up work, social skills classes, groups to motivate pupils who have poor attendance or who are at risk of exclusion (Hallam 1996). There are many possibilities. Specific groups can be run alongside normal curriculum classes to offer integrated provision for pupils with moderate to severe learning difficulties (Ireson 1999). Groups may also be run outside school hours to support learning or develop further skills (Sharp *et al.* 1999). The main advantage of groups set up for special activities is their flexibility. Whether they are set up to withdraw pupils from curriculum subjects, are on offer in the lunch hour or after school, or are timetabled as special activities they offer flexibility that other methods of structuring groupings do not. They can be offered for short periods of time to satisfy particular needs without disruption to the whole school timetable.

Teacher skills

As we saw in Chapter 4, teachers find it easier to teach and manage classes that are grouped by ability. Successful mixed-ability teaching relies heavily on teacher skills (Reid *et al.* 1982). Teachers need to be flexible, use a variety of teaching modes in one lesson, vary the pace and style of approach, use a range of audio-visual media and encourage a variety of pupil activities. They need to be able to develop informal relationships with their pupils, involve pupils in decision making and engage them in learning activities (Kerry & Sands 1984). To successfully teach mixed-ability classes teachers need access to appropriate resources and facilities. These have not always been available and teachers have often had to spend a great deal of time developing differentiated materials for teaching.

Planning

If particular activities are to be effective in promoting learning, teachers need to plan carefully taking into account a range of issues. First, they need to consider the aims and objectives of the activity or task they are setting. While these are usually expressed in academic terms, considering how they will affect the personal and social educational outcomes for pupils is also important. The development of personal and social skills supports academic development and in the long term is crucial to pupil performance. For instance, if pupils learn to be critical of their work, this is likely to lead to higher standards. If they learn how to improve their concentration this will have positive benefits for work across the curriculum. If their social skills are improved they will be better able to support each other in academic work, behaviour will improve, increasing time on task and the working climate within the classroom will be more positive. Teachers need to achieve a balance between whole-class, large and small group, paired and individual work for pupils, balancing the maximisation of expert teacher input with providing opportunities for pupils to work independently, alone or with others. Offering a variety of different learning opportunities not only promotes the development of the 'whole' child but also takes account of individual differences in learning styles. Working in different ways also provides variety for pupils, reducing the possibility of boredom.

The allocation of pupils to groups needs to be made with care. This will be considered in relation to ability groups in the next chapter. Mixed-ability groups should include the whole range of ability, be balanced for gender and, where appropriate, age and ethnicity. Pupils require group allocations for numeracy, literacy and mixed-ability work. The groups for numeracy and literacy, which are essentially for teaching purposes, will be larger than those where pupils are expected to work collaboratively. The latter should never include more than six children. Group allocations for literacy and numeracy are likely to be different as children usually exhibit very different levels of attainment in these domains. Seating allocations for individual and paired work, particularly if a U shape layout is adopted, may be left to pupil choice, as the seating arrangements, of themselves, automatically give the teacher greater control. However, there may be some circumstances where teachers feel the need to determine seating, for instance, where particular children need to be kept apart.

To summarise, when making decisions about grouping in any particular teaching session teachers need to ask themselves a series of questions:

- What learning outcomes are to be attained in this session (including academic, personal, social)?

- What teaching methods and tasks are most appropriate to attain these outcomes?
- What type or combination of pupil grouping will best support the teaching methods and task (whole class, ability groups, mixed-ability groups, pairs, individual work)?
- How can I best allocate individual pupils to groups to promote motivation to learn and enhance time on task to assist in the attainment of these learning outcomes?

Following the session they should ask:

- How successful have the teaching method, task and grouping strategies been in attaining the desired learning outcomes?
- Am I providing a sufficiently varied range of learning and grouping experiences to promote pupils' motivation and interest?

The evaluations of each session, particularly information about what was successful and what was not, then feed into the planning process for subsequent sessions.

Conclusion

In the primary school, mixed-ability classes offer flexibility. They enable teachers to move pupils between groups as their learning needs change more easily than when groupings are structured by ability. Teaching can be focused at the level of the class or large group, while work can be set at the individual, paired or group level. This provides pupils with varied opportunities for learning which not only take account of individual learning styles but also facilitate the development of personal and social skills. Where pupils are to work collaboratively in small groups or pairs, they require guidance as to what behaviours are expected and are acceptable. As these social skills are developed, the working environment of the classroom should be enhanced with positive benefits for pupils and teachers. For this to occur, teachers need to plan activities and the grouping structures within which they are to be implemented carefully.

Chapter summary: mixed-ability and within-class groupings

Mixed-ability classes offer greater flexibility in grouping pupils than structured ability groupings.

The opportunity to adopt different groupings within the class can facilitate the development of pupils' academic, personal and social skills.

The successful operation of within-class groupings requires:

- An appropriate physical environment;
- Planning;
- Effective organisation;
- Careful allocation of pupils to groups;
- Clearly defined tasks and learning outcomes; and
- Guidance for pupils on how to work in collaborative groups.

Further reading

Croll, P. & Hastings, N. (eds) (1996) *Effective primary teaching: research-based classroom strategies*. London: David Fulton Publishers.

Galton, M. & Williamson, J. (1992) *Groupwork in the primary classroom*. London: Routledge.

Kutnick, P. & Rogers, C. (eds) (1994) *Groups in schools*. London: Cassell.

Chapter 6

The management of ability and mixed-ability groups in schools

Introduction

This chapter considers how pupils are allocated to ability and mixed-ability groups, how the effectiveness of groupings is monitored and how movement between groups is managed. For grouping practices to be effective, initial group placement needs to be based on the child's current level of attainment with the possibility of movement to a higher or lower group should the rate of progress change. In practice, as we shall see, allocation to groups is often based on factors unrelated to current attainment while there is very little movement between groups.

The allocation of pupils to ability groups

Historically, the allocation of pupils to streams or sets has been a somewhat arbitrary affair, not based entirely on prior academic achievement or ability (Ireson & Hallam 2001). Even now, some schools use no objective or consistent measures when allocating pupils to groups, which greatly increases the possibility of a mismatch between a pupil's placement and their ability (Sukhnandan & Lee 1998). When streaming was commonplace in UK primary schools, Barker Lunn (1970) showed that 15 per cent of children were in the wrong stream at the end of the school year on the basis of English and arithmetic performance. This percentage was lower in the early primary years and higher in the later years. At the beginning of the next school year, on average a quarter of these children were moved into their correct stream, but three quarters remained in the wrong stream given their test performance. Children remaining in too high a stream tended to improve but those in too low a stream tended to deteriorate. Those in too low a stream were often the younger pupils in the year group and those in too high a stream the older. Such inappropriate allocation of pupils to groups continues today. There is often considerable overlap in test scores between pupils in the lower-ability groups and those in middle groups. In some cases, overlap has been found between those pupils in the lower groups and those in the top groups (MacIntyre & Ireson 2002).

Usually there is consensus between standardised test or attainment results, and teachers' perceptions and judgements about group alloca-tion (Troman 1988). Where this is not the case, teachers tend to rely on their perceptions of pupils. They take into account pupils' prior performance, knowledge of the attainment of brothers and sisters, previous grouping allocations and even pupils' physical appearance. Reading group placements in the first year of schooling are not always based on children's academic performance, potential or background (Pallas *et al.* 1994). Other factors perceived as important within the school are taken into account. In some cases children exhibiting poor behaviour or motivation are allocated to lower-ability groups. In other instances schools try to separate disruptive pupils, which can also lead to inappropriate set placement (Ireson & Hallam 2001). Once placed in a group, because movement is restricted, inequalities in children's academic achievement over a period of several years can become greater (Dreeben & Barr 1988; Reuman 1989).

Grouping allocation, to a great extent, determines the learning opportunities available to pupils. Tiered entry to national attainment tests and external examinations depends largely on a child's grouping placement. Inappropriate group allocation at primary school can have far reaching effects on a child's future prospects because of the relative lack of movement between groups. A child placed in a low-ability group early in their school career is unlikely to rise to a top-ability group, even if the original allocation was inaccurate.

Current practices in allocating pupils to groups

Many schools implementing ability grouping rely heavily on data derived from standardised testing to allocate pupils to groups. These tests can discriminate against minority groups. While they attempt to test potential through exploring performance on abstract tasks, the materials they use are more familiar to some pupils than others. Richardson (1991) demonstrated that when logical reasoning tasks were presented in familiar contexts, for instance using food, cars or sporting scenes, pupils performed significantly better than when abstract shapes were used. For this reason, the use of standardised tests has been banned in many states in the United States. Apportioning educational opportunity through performance on standardised tests can also mean allocating very different educational opportunities on the basis of a one mark difference. Tests currently used to allocate pupils to groups tend to be national attainment tests or those measuring aspects of cognitive ability. Where schools adopt rigorous ability grouping structures, they tend to rely heavily on testing procedures. An example is given in Box 6.1.

School 1 is a large primary school where pupils are streamed upon entry into one 'fast track' class and two mixed-ability classes. The children who are perceived as being more able on the basis of their baseline test results receive an accelerated curriculum in comparison to the other two classes. In Key Stage 2, the children are reorganised into mixed-ability classes but are then set for the core curriculum subjects. Pupils' performance on tests is used as the basis for decisions made about their placement:

> We use statistical data because we test the children – in January we do NFER testing, we do SATs at the end of every year. In Key Stage 1 we have banks of assessment tests and tasks, and we make judgements about where children should be in relation to all of the statistical data. We never make judgements on the basis of 'Oh I think he can . . .' (Head teacher)

Box 6.1   The use of testing

The use of testing is regarded by many schools to be a reliable source of information on which to base a pupil's allocation to a particular ability group. However, the use of testing is controversial.

Difficulties associated with the use of testing

There are debates about the extent to which tests are valid and reliable indicators of ability (see Howe 1997 or Richardson 1999 for discussions of the issues). Questions have also been raised about the extent to which attainment tests accurately assess pupils' understanding and knowledge and suitability for placement in a particular group. For instance, pupils may perform well in a test but may not respond well to the faster pace and higher expectations characteristic of higher-ability groups. Pupils may perform poorly on a test because of a mismatch between their written skills and understanding of a particular concept. For other pupils, the relatively artificial nature of the testing situation and their lack of familiarity with it may lead to underperformance. Tests provide only a snapshot in time, they do not take into consideration sudden 'spurts' in cognitive development or 'lightbulb' moments, while overall test performance scores can obscure strengths and weaknesses within a subject, as one teacher indicated:

> I tend to find that children have a different level of ability within maths – some are spatially very strong, some are very good with numbers and so even the setting system isn't fluid enough – you've got some children all the time that are going to go up and down in different topics. (Mathematics coordinator, school 4)

Testing also has personal and social consequences. Poor performance in a test can have an impact on children's self-esteem and lead to negative perceptions of themselves as learners. Too great an emphasis on tests can lead to the adoption of a narrow conception of learning, particularly where teaching focuses on test performance. Tests can also be culturally biased and deny opportunities for pupils from ethnic minorities to demonstrate their abilities.

Despite these potential difficulties, the use of testing is very much a part of the current UK education system. Pupils face baseline assessment upon entry to schools and statutory end of key stage national tests. More and more schools have introduced non-statutory national tests, particularly in Key Stage 2 classes so that pupils are prepared for the year 6 tests which will impact upon the school's performance data and subsequent league table position. In order to address some of the shortfalls of test-derived data, some schools have supplemented it with other information. This practice is supported by Ofsted (1998b), who have indicated that schools should take into account factors such as pupils' interest in, or aptitude for, a subject which may not be revealed by testing. In the process of assigning a pupil to an ability group, schools need to collate as much information as possible to make an effective judgement, as one teacher explained:

> The quality of the data which is used to split them [into ability streams] isn't that high . . . we do also get together and discuss whether we think that they could handle a particular group, their maturity levels, whether some might relate better to a male teacher as opposed to a female teacher . . . issues like that. (Deputy head teacher, school 2)

In some schools, lack of prior knowledge of pupils' learning has determined the year in which ability grouping has been implemented, allowing teachers to gather further information about pupils. For example:

> We need to get to know what they have done and also, more importantly than 'what', we're looking at 'how' they work because in our top maths set there's a lot of abstract thinking. So we monitor them all through their first year and at the end we do a test set by teachers of the work they have covered in class and an NFER test as well. Then I will meet with all my year 3 teachers and my head of maths, so there'll be five of us, and we'll sit down and go through every child and put them into groups. (Head teacher, school 4)

Summary   *placed in wrong groups*

The decision processes involved in allocating pupils to ability groups are complex. Tests alone rarely provide sufficient information upon which to make decisions about a child's assignment to a particular group. Test data needs to be supplemented with additional information. This has implications for staff time. The potential for a pupil to be wrongly allocated to an ability group is very high. For this reason schools' assessment procedures need to be developed with a particular emphasis on providing accurate and full information to assist in the appropriate allocation of pupils to groups.

Allocation of pupils to mixed-ability teaching groups

As we saw in Chapter 2, the use of ability grouping has increased in recent years and all children now spend at least part of their school day in a group that is made up of children of similar ability. Schools also implement mixed-ability or friendship groupings for some subjects – some believing that this counteracts the negative effects of ability grouping in other curriculum areas, particularly for those children in the lower-ability groups. To promote effective mixed-ability work the allocation of pupils to groups requires careful consideration. Teachers need to monitor group processes and performance to ensure that the groups are operating successfully.

As was outlined in the previous chapter, groups should have a balance of gender, ethnicity, ability and, where appropriate, age. To ensure that all groups are appropriately constructed, group allocation will require teacher direction, otherwise opportunities for social mixing and personal development will be missed.

If teachers provide guidance to pupils on how to work effectively in groups, most will learn to work together cooperatively. However, teachers will need to monitor the extent to which there is a positive and purposeful working atmosphere in each group and where necessary intervene, either to change group membership or assist the group in working together more successfully. For example:

> It's got to be a workable group and that tends to be my main focus – to put children into groups that will work well together. I tend to mix the sexes up and I tend to keep friendships apart as I want them to socialise with children that they don't normally socialise with to enhance those skills as well . . . if I don't want to specifically group according to ability, then I would split them up and they'd move around. On the whole though, I am thinking of good working groups that will remain on task. (Key Stage 2 teacher, school 4)

Even where the group is working well together it may be necessary for the teacher to monitor the extent to which each pupil has the opportunity to take on different roles, e.g. to collect data, record findings, present findings. Group placement for the literacy and numeracy hours can help to ensure that genuine mixed-ability groups are formed. One Key Stage 2 teacher described her practice as follows:

> In science we have mixed-ability groups and I form those by taking the ability groupings from the literacy hour. I put each of the top ability at a table and spread them across the class so that I know that there is at least one above-average child on each table so that the level of discussion can be higher and less able children can be helped and supported. I think that this is a good way of raising standards. (School 6)

Teachers have to decide whether the allocation of able pupils should be made on the basis of literacy or numeracy. Whichever choice is made it is crucial that each mixed-ability group has at least one able child and a spread of ability.

Behaviour and group allocation

Pupil behaviour, as we saw in the previous chapter, is often taken into account when pupils are allocated to groups. Teachers need to ensure that any single group does not have an over-representation of pupils whose behaviour is likely to be problematic. This applies equally to groups based on ability or mixed-ability. Box 6.2 gives an example of how one school addressed this issue in relation to ability groups.

In school 1 steps are taken to avoid the creation of groups with an over-representation of pupils with behavioural problems. For one particular cohort of pupils, adopting the usual procedure of allocating pupils to sets for the core curriculum according to their performance on tests meant that the lowest-ability group was considered to be unmanageable. To avoid this, the school created two parallel sets so that more challenging pupils could be equally distributed between the two. Although this increased the ability range in each set, the benefits in terms of behaviour were seen to compensate:

We're now at a stage where we can say that a child will not be in a particular group because of behaviour. You know there are certain times when you're grouping children according to ability and you suddenly realise that you've got a potential dynamite group – they're going to be so lively. We take these things into consideration and perhaps run sets as parallels. We do that so children who are known to have a friction between other children are given that little bit of space apart. (English coordinator)

Box 6.2   Ensuring that good behaviour is maintained

This school was fortunate in being larger than average, well resourced, with generous staffing levels, enabling considerable flexibility in grouping-related decisions. Other schools may need to adopt different strategies to ensure that problems that may result from poor behaviour are minimised.

Group size

One frequently cited advantage of adopting structured ability grouping for all or part of the curriculum is that it facilitates the creation of smaller teaching groups, particularly for less able pupils. This assists in meeting pupils' needs and increases the level of pupil–teacher inter-actions. However, in practice, this is not always possible. Schools sometimes find themselves playing a 'numbers' game. An example is given in Box 6.3.

In school 3, the aim is to maintain a very small lower-ability class to ensure that individual needs can be met. This plan has had to be abandoned in the light of changing circumstances:

We had the idea that we would always have lower numbers at the lower end, but the gaps further up are filling. So I've now had an issue already raised by the year 5–6 teacher who has the lower-ability class. He has had six new children join since September, all with SEN that I couldn't put in any other class, and he now has rising numbers and feels that he is unable to provide what the children need. The other two teachers are saying that they have 32 and 33 children. I've tried to outline that the lower-ability group should not go over 25, that you have to accept that the other classes become bigger. But the other point is do you put children in that ability group that genuinely need to be there or, whenever you get to the borderline, you have to think if children can really keep up with the work of the middle or upper groups. So do you place children according to their needs or are we playing a numbers game? That's an issue that you can't escape really. (Head teacher)

Box 6.3 Coping with different ratios of able and less able pupils

The monitoring of grouping practices

The monitoring of grouping practices has two strands. The first is the monitoring of the placement of individual pupils to a particular group. The second is the monitoring of the effectiveness of grouping strategies across the whole school or key stage. Relevant questions to be addressed in relation to the second of these include:

- Are the grouping practices achieving what they set out to achieve?
- Are there any negative consequences of the implementation of particular grouping practices?
- How can the grouping practices be improved?

Establishing the success, or otherwise, of particular grouping strategies requires that the arrangements in place are monitored and evaluated. On the basis of the outcomes of these processes schools need to be sufficiently flexible to be able to implement changes should they be necessary. The monitoring and evaluation systems need to be an integral part of school policy and practice. As one deputy head described, schools need to constantly strive for improvement:

It's really important to know that nothing is set in stone . . . that's the only way that an establishment can grow . . . the minute you start to think that you've got all the answers, things start to decline. I still think that there are things that we can do to make things better for the children. (Deputy head teacher, school 1)

Ways that schools can monitor and evaluate the effectiveness of grouping practices are set out in Box 6.4. Adoption of a range of practices, in this way, can ensure that individual group allocation is appropriate and also that groups work effectively to optimise pupil learning. In monitoring the effectiveness of policies schools also need to take into account practical issues, for example, the extent to which the school layout enables the easy movement of groups of children around the building when they are moving between ability grouped classes. Practices will be enhanced if:

- non-contact time can be made available for class-based staff in order for in-depth analysis and follow up to take place;
- pupil allocation to groups is a prominent feature of the School Development Plan, which is regularly discussed;
- a pupil's allocation to a particular group is a feature of an Individual Educational Plan (IEP) or included in termly target setting.

Schools can monitor and evaluate the effectiveness of their grouping policies and practices through:

- the analysis of group composition in terms of gender, ethnicity, ability, age and behaviour;
- whole-school reviews of schemes of work;
- involvement of LEA advisers;
- the collection and analysis of samples of children's work;
- the analysis of test results;
- teachers' professional judgements informed by interactions with and observations of groups at work;
- discussions with pupils about their experiences of grouping;
- discussions with parents.

Box 6.4 Methods for monitoring and evaluating the effectiveness of grouping strategies

Obstacles to effective monitoring of grouping practices

There are a number of factors that can limit the extent to which schools can effectively develop, implement and monitor their grouping practices.

These include lack of time, pressure on staff, school size, lack of priority for grouping issues and an over-emphasis on test results.

Lack of time – in an already over-crowded school day, it is possible for the best intentions not to be realised because of more pressing matters, particularly in schools facing inspections or staff shortages.

Pressure on staff – in order for effective and meaningful development, implementation and monitoring of grouping practices to take place, class teachers need non-contact time to meet with colleagues and to analyse and consider individual pupils' progress. This is not always possible.

School size – primary schools vary enormously in terms of their pupil numbers. Effective monitoring may be more difficult in large schools as there may be insufficient time available to consider all pupils' needs in a meaningful way. Schools need to develop strategies that work for them according to the resources that they have available. (See Boxes 6.5 and 6.6 for examples of monitoring in small and large schools.)

Lack of priority for grouping issues – in order for development, implementation and monitoring to be taken seriously, there is the need for a whole-school commitment. Effective monitoring is much more difficult if there is not a consensus of opinion regarding its importance or regarding the type of grouping strategy being implemented. This clearly has implications for schools with high staff mobility or recruitment difficulties.

In school 5, a small school, monitoring takes place regularly in staff meetings:

Well, we have a planning meeting and on a Monday we have five minutes when we just get together and go through the week's plans for everybody. Then on a Friday night, we have 15 minutes at the end of the week to have a look at how that's all worked. Then we do group assessments and individual assessments so that we can feed back on any areas that are new or anything that's changed. We have a look at how the groups are going and we collect material to substantiate whether we think it's working or not and then we feed that back to each other. At the end of the term we do a re-cap of everything that we've done and we just find out whether it's worked or not. If there's a blip in the middle [of the term], as long as we've got something to substantiate what we say, then we'll alter it in the middle, but usually, it's at the end of the term or half term where we'll have one long session where we'll go through everything and just look at what's right and what's wrong and alter where we think we can alter. (Head teacher)

Box 6.5   Monitoring grouping in a small school

Over-emphasis on data derived from tests – where teachers consider test-derived data to be the only accurate source of information to use for grouping pupils, the need for regular monitoring is often overlooked. Schools need to recognise that tests may not provide the whole picture and that some pupils' needs may not be revealed through testing. Monitoring of pupils' progress in other ways then becomes crucial.

Box 6.6 provides an example of the process of monitoring in a large school that adopts structured ability grouping. Opportunities for informal interaction between staff are relatively rare because of the size of the school. One member of staff was therefore given the responsibility for monitoring the effectiveness of groupings across the school.

Where pupils are grouped within classes, less formal monitoring often takes place, and the process relies to a greater extent on teacher judgement. As one Key Stage 1 teacher described, teachers may take account of behaviour, work output and their own interactions with, and observations of pupils in, different grouping situations:

> I just tend to monitor them through the outcomes of the group in terms of their behaviour and the work they do. It is quite clear if there are children who are sitting together and shouldn't be in terms of how chatty they are or if they distract each other. (School 6)

In school 1:

> There is one person in school who is responsible for standards and effectiveness in the school and she has just finished collecting the books from the whole school in maths, English and science and she has done an analysis, a very detailed analysis of what's going on and where there might be any room for improvement. This happens every half term. Not only does that person look at the books, but also the year coordinators have a responsibility to monitor the books within their year groups so there's very close monitoring and evaluation that goes on all the time by various people in the school who communicate and feed back to each other. (Head teacher)

The mathematics coordinator illustrates how this monitoring might impact upon a pupil's placement in a particular group:

> . . . our teachers and management team are experts in looking out for tell-tale signs that a child might be unhappy or feel pressurised and they know that the system isn't rigid – they can change groups and I think that is so important.

Box 6.6 Monitoring of ability grouping in a large school

The need for the teacher's active participation in groups in order for this assessment to take place is an important element that can inform professional judgement. For example:

> I think that basically the way I do it is that I participate with the groups – I can't just sit at my desk and let them get on with it – I have to be a part of it. I listen to the views being shared and you can always tell if there's someone who's not particularly forthcoming with their views and comments, in which case you'd know that next time that person might be better off in a different group, perhaps with a friend in order to give them more confidence . . . observation as well as participation. (Key Stage 2 teacher, school 4)

Overall, taking decisions about grouping arrangements is complex. Monitoring of the effectiveness of current policies and practices needs to be viewed as a continual process. Box 6.7 provides an illustration of this.

When concerns arise about the effectiveness of a particular grouping practice, whole-school decisions may need to be taken, possibly resulting in major changes or restructuring of grouping arrangements. In addition, monitoring must be undertaken to ensure that pupils are

---

In response to a critical Ofsted report, one of the survey schools piloted the use of setting for literacy and numeracy in an attempt to raise its standards. Staff were committed to try the policy for a period of two years. During this time, pupils' performance on national tests, behaviour, and the feelings of teachers, were considered. At the end of the pilot period, the senior management team met with teachers and parents and engaged in lengthy discussions and analyses of available data. It was felt by some that, although test results had improved, the improvement was not sufficient to justify the negative impact in other areas. Some teachers were concerned specifically about the access that less able pupils had to appropriate role models, the behaviour of the less able groups, and the disruption caused to the school day due to the movement of pupils around the school building. Some teachers felt that they were unable to keep track of the progress of individual pupils in their classes due to insufficient time to meet with teachers working with the pupils in sets. Other teachers felt that the use of setting was positive and that the raising of attainment in national tests, particularly of the more able pupils, coupled with the reduction in the range of abilities to be catered for within a class was enough to justify the continuation of the practice. After much debate, a compromise was reached with setting being continued for numeracy and abandoned for literacy.

Box 6.7   Decision making about grouping strategies

appropriately allocated to groups and that, when necessary, they are moved between them.

Movement between groups

Although in theory movement between structured ability groups is possible, it is often limited, particularly where streaming is in operation (Barker Lunn 1970; Devine 1993). The importance of pupils being able to move sets is stressed as crucial for the successful operation of structured grouping systems (Ofsted 1998b) but in practice there is usually very little movement. This was confirmed by comments made by staff in the case study schools. Some examples are given below.

> Moving between sets hasn't really happened much so far really – we're still getting used to it. (Key Stage 2 teacher, school 3)

> We don't change a lot of children because it's going to be hopeless if we were always changing children's groups. Usually, I try to only change them once a year unless something happens where a child changes dramatically. (Head teacher, school 4)

In at least one case study school, the lack of opportunity for pupils to change ability groups was seen as a problem:

> I think one of the problems, and it's something that we're trying to address more recently, is the rigidity of set class placement – a child goes into a particular set and is seen as in that position for life! We do want to move away from that, and I think that probably once we've established a much stronger system then people can move and it's seen as being a much more fluid system. (Mathematics coordinator, school 4)

There is evidence that pupils are not moved between groups, even when teachers are aware that pupils are wrongly allocated (Barker Lunn 1970, Troyna 1992). One problem is that there is often a gap between work that has been undertaken and what is required in a higher group. A further problem is that in order to move some pupils to a higher group others have to move down (Ireson & Hallam 2001). Where children do change group, if the movement is in an upward direction they tend to do better, but if it is in a downward direction they tend to do worse (Barker

Lunn 1970). Pupils tend to conform to the standard of the group to which they are allocated.

In a study of within-class grouping for reading, Barr (1995) noted that on entry to primary school children differed enormously in their reading experience. Children with little experience needed more practice to catch up with their peers, but they were not usually given extra time for this in school. They generally took longer to finish the first book in a reading scheme, but then proceeded at a similar pace to others. When the focus of reading moved on to comprehension, teachers tended not to regroup the children, leaving many incorrectly placed. Incorrect placement in ability groups may therefore have long-term consequences for pupils' learning. Pupils tend to move groups less in formalised ability grouping situations, e.g. setting and streaming, and more when they are grouped within classes. Movement between groups is facilitated when:

- Grouping practices are viewed as flexible and pupils' progress is monitored regularly. This is more likely to occur where there is a whole-school commitment to moving pupils and monitoring their progress;
- Teachers are allocated time specifically for considering the progress of individual pupils within groups;
- Pupils and parents know that the school is committed to movement between groups and there is evidence of this in practice. This may also reduce pressure from parents;
- There is close coordination of schemes of work and curricula taught to different ability groups to ensure that gaps in pupils' learning are minimal. This has been facilitated by the introduction of the national literacy and numeracy strategies;
- The issue of grouping has a high profile within the school and is raised in relation to target setting and IEPs.

Where pupils are ability grouped within classes for particular subjects, movement between groups is easier to achieve. Teachers can monitor pupil progress and group placement on a daily basis and make changes when they judge it to be necessary. For example:

This term so far, I have moved some children for maths . . . some were finding it too easy and some were struggling . . . I think at this age, children might have spurts and there might be times when they suddenly find things really easy, so you have to keep an eye on things. The groups aren't fixed though . . . it depends on the children's progress. (Key Stage 1 teacher, school 6)

Within-class ability grouping offers more flexibility and ease in relation to pupil movement between groups than either setting or streaming.

Parental pressure

Parents often express concern about the groups that their children are assigned to in school, particularly when schools are adopting more formal ability groupings such as setting. This section describes how parents can react to children's grouping allocation and what schools can do to develop positive strategies to justify their actions to parents. Naturally, parents want the best for their children and mismatches can often arise between parents' perceptions of their children's ability and the perceptions of the school. One teacher described:

Sometimes it's the perception that the parents have of their child as well. Every parent's child is wonderful, that is the most difficult thing – to be tactful when you're telling them that perhaps they're not totally right in their appraisal of their child. (Head teacher, school 5)

In several of the case study schools, head teachers took on the task of communicating with parents regarding the allocation and movement of their offspring between ability groups because of the level of parental pressure:

There is a vast amount of parental pressure! I try always to do it from my perspective because the teachers have enough to deal with, with all the work they're doing without parents saying, 'I want my child to do this or that.' So, for things like that, I always send things out with my name at the bottom. If they want to say anything, then they can come in here and see me. I mean, I'm a parent, I know what it's like and you have to say, 'I will monitor your child, I will watch your child.' I keep in my diary things where I do monitor them. If there are children that I want to check, then I'll put them in the diary and I'll monitor them to see what I feel that I'm going to do about them. I think that if parents see that and see that you're doing all you can, then they're happy with that. (Head teacher, school 4)

Schools indicated the importance of being able to explain clearly to parents why the child is being moved and being able to provide evidence to support the decision. Teachers also need to be tactful, demonstrate understanding of the parents' perspective and provide a clear rationale for the change. Two head teachers provide examples:

I've had quite a few parents whose children have been moved down coming in and saying that they are unhappy about it, but usually when you explain it all to them they do accept it. If we say that it's for the child's benefit and that they'll work better in a different set we don't usually get any more problems. They usually accept what we say but they do come in. (School 1)

When the decisions were made, I stayed one evening and I rang every parent direct and I said, 'Having looked at the way they're working and having looked at their results, we've decided to move your child.' Having spoken to all the parents, there was only one who said, 'You can't do that!' and it was a set 1 to set 2 move, and I said, 'I can do it, but I don't want us to do it with bad feeling. I want us to talk it through and see why.' The parent wanted time to do extra work with the child at home and I said, 'Look, your child's a set 1 child – working fast, abstract thinking, a lot of work to do. Set 2 is covering exactly the same programme but in a different way.' 'But I don't want my child in set 2,' she said. So I said, 'But what about the 5 children in set 2 that I'm having to hold back because there's no room in set 1? What about them?' Then the parent said, 'Well, all right, I see.' We agreed to move the child into set 2 with the assurance that if I found that the child was just being lazy, but could really cope with the set 1 work, then in September I'd move her back. You've got to give them a lifeline. You can't leave them thinking, 'Gosh, whatever she says, there's no changing her mind,' because I don't think that's fair. (School 4)

Whatever the systems that schools have in place, the issue of pupil allocation to groups can still be an emotive one for parents. Schools need to have a clear rationale in order to be able to justify decisions regarding the grouping of pupils. The need for consistency across the school is also important in order to instil confidence in pupils and parents regarding the decision-making processes within the school. This can be undermined if pupils perceive that their parents have been influential in instigating changes in their group allocation. For example:

> Well, my dad talked to the head teacher and then they moved me up and I felt pleased because I wasn't with the people I didn't like very much and I felt that I was moving up to my level. (Pupil, school 3)

Parents' concerns are not restricted to the school's assessment of their children's ability but can also relate to social issues, for example a request that their child be with a particular friend or be separated from some individuals. Teachers and schools need to be prepared to address such concerns and be able to justify their decisions. There is a need for schools to develop whole-school strategies based on principles agreed jointly by staff. Box 6.8 sets out how schools might effectively reassure parents.

To reassure parents schools need:

- clearly defined grouping policies and practices;
- clear and consistent rationales for allocating pupils to ability groups;
- to communicate information about grouping practices in school documentation;
- clear procedures for communicating decisions about a child's group placement to parents and pupils;
- clear evidence of why pupils are allocated to particular groups and evidence of the monitoring of each child's progress within a particular group; and
- opportunities for parents to contribute to reviews of grouping policies.

Box 6.8   Dealing with parental concerns regarding pupil allocation to and movement between groups

Conclusion

Decisions regarding the allocation, monitoring and movement of pupils between ability groups are complex. Schools considering the adoption of particular grouping strategies, particularly those based on pupils' perceived ability, need to be aware of these issues and have policies and practices in place that have been developed by the whole school staff and have their full support. There is considerable evidence that pupils are frequently allocated to an inappropriate ability group. As movement between groups is limited, this can have long-term implications for pupils' future educational performance, their percep-tions of themselves as learners and their lifelong view of education and schooling. The evidence also suggests that some groups of pupils are over-represented in the lower-ability groups. This has implications for society as particular groups may be denied equal educational oppor-tunities. Schools need to do everything in their power to ensure that group placement is fair and based on prior attainment and that there is easily manageable movement between groups.

Chapter summary: The management of ability and mixed-ability groups in schools

The allocation of pupils to ability groups is a complex process.

It should not rely exclusively on standardised testing or attainment but needs to take account of how pupils will respond to particular ways of working without disadvantaging their progress.

Grouping policies and practices should be developed in consultation with all staff and time needs to be allocated for discussion of grouping placements and movement between groups.

Grouping policies and practices need to be communicated to parents.

Pupils' group placements should be monitored and opportunities provided for frequent movement between groups so that children are not disadvantaged by their group placement.

Clear and consistent channels of communication need to be estab-lished between the school and parents. Information about their child's placement needs to be handled sensitively, providing them with the evidence on which decisions have been made.

Schools need to ensure that particular groups within the school population are not disadvantaged by grouping procedures.

Grouping strategies should be monitored and evaluated in the light of evidence and changed when necessary.

Further reading

Harlen, W. & Malcolm, H. (1997) *Setting and streaming: a research review* (Using Research Series 18). Edinburgh: SCRE.

Howe, M. J. A. (1997) *IQ in question: the truth about intelligence.* London: Sage.

Richardson, K. (1999) *The making of intelligence.* London: Weidenfeld and Nicolson.

Sukhnandan, L. & Lee, B. (1998) *Streaming, setting and grouping by ability: a review of the literature.* Slough: NFER.

Chapter 7

Overview and conclusions

Education for the twenty-first century

Schools in the UK were developed during an industrial age to satisfy the needs of society at that time (Bayliss 1998), a society which was more rigid in its structures – class, gender roles, religious identity – and working practices. Society is now multicultural, class and religion play a smaller part in the identity-formation of most people and gender roles have changed considerably. The nature of work has also changed. Manufacturing industry in the UK continues to decline while there has been an increase in service industries and their availability to customers. As a consequence, there are fewer unskilled employment opportunities and a rising demand for a better educated workforce that is literate, numerate and skilled in information processing. Working practices have generally become less rigid with flexi-working hours, more choice of when to take lunch, breaks and holidays, more part-time and hourly-paid work and more working from home. These changes in working patterns have not been reflected in school structures and practices. Most schools operate during fixed hours that have not taken account of changes in the patterns of parental employment, particularly the increased number of women working, and holidays continue to be planned around the need to bring in the harvest. During the last 15 years much government guidance and legislation has reintroduced practices that were in place at the beginning of the twentieth century, e.g. national testing, structured ability grouping, increased levels of homework, payment of teachers by results. Schools are attempting to provide education for the changing needs of the twenty-first century in structures designed for the greater rigidity of the nineteenth century. It is clear that more flexibility is required. Nowhere is this more important than in relation to the grouping of pupils.

The aims of education

Whether alternative forms of grouping are seen as effective or not depends on the definition of effectiveness adopted and the criteria against which it is assessed. These are rightly the subject of public and political debate. Views of 'effectiveness' change over time in relation to national priorities. Without clearly defined guidelines as to what is expected of education, the pursuit of 'effective' practice in schools is problematic. While the original version of the National Curriculum did not include educational aims, the most recent formulation (DfEE/ QCA 1999), as we saw in Chapter 1, sets out clearly the values and purposes underpinning education in the UK. There is an acknowledgement that education has a role to play in influencing the values and nature of society, and in providing the basis for the spiritual, moral, social, cultural, physical and mental development of the individual, i.e. their well-being. Education is acknowledged to be a route to 'equality of opportunity for all, a healthy and just democracy, a productive economy, and sustainable development' (1999: 10). As we have seen in the earlier chapters of this book, highly structured ability grouping tends not to satisfy these aims and it can have negative effects on the well-being of some children, also restricting their academic development.

The aims of the National Curriculum also require that pupils be prepared to respond to the 'opportunities and challenges of the rapidly changing world in which we live and work' (1999: 10). This requires learners to be flexible and adaptable, and to be prepared and willing to engage with education beyond the years of compulsory schooling. A range of transferable skills that can be applied in different employment circumstances need to be learned – not only academic skills but teamwork, planning, knowing how to learn and having the confidence to do so. Rigid ability grouping structures, as they tend to be practised, do not provide all children with the opportunities to develop these skills.

Changing conceptions of intelligence

Underlying all structured grouping policies are fundamental assumptions relating to the nature of intelligence. Historically, there has been an assumption that pupils have different levels of 'ability' which are genetically based, relatively immutable and unchanging. This perception developed from early conceptions of the nature of intelligence and its measurement through IQ (Intelligence Quotient) tests. Recent research evidence has challenged these ideas, suggesting that intelligence is not a single entity. Further, there is consensus among the research community that the environment is crucial to its development. In other words, much of what we describe as intelligence is learned.

Modern theories share the view that intelligence is complex and multi-faceted. Where they differ is in their conceptualisations of the nature of this complexity. Gardner's (1993, 1999) theory of multiple intelligences suggests that there are nine separate intelligences: linguistic, logico-mathematical, spatial, musical, bodily-kinaesthetic, interpersonal, intra-personal, naturalist and spiritual/existential. Sternberg's (1984) triarchic theory adopts a different approach. He considers intelligence as it relates to the internal world of the individual, specifically the mechan-isms that underlie intelligent behaviour, our thought processes; as it relates to the external world of the individual, specifically the use of these mechanisms in everyday life in order to 'fit' into the environment; and intelligence and experience, specifically how what one learns in life mediates between the internal and external worlds of the individual. Ceci (1990) proposes a bio-ecological theory, which like Gardner's is based on an assumption of multiple intelligences. He stresses the importance of the environment in the development of intelligence including motivational forces, the social and physical aspects of a particular learning environment or task and the subject domain in which the task is embedded. Knowledge and ability are viewed as fundamentally inseparable. In other words ability is merely a reflection of what the individual has learnt in the past. Recently, others have suggested that even within single subject domains individuals may have different strengths and weaknesses (Hallam 1998). This was reflected by a teacher from one of the case study schools who pointed out that pupils could perform quite differently in spatial and number skills within mathematics.

Performance and the outcomes of learning do not depend on 'intelli-gence' but on the complex interactions of many factors. These include the characteristics of the learning situation, motivation, effort, belief in the possibility of success, opportunity, knowledge of learning strategies, self-awareness and prior knowledge in addition to ability (Biggs & Moore 1993; Hallam & Ireson 1999). Overall, intelligence, as tradition-ally conceived, is now believed to play a relatively small part in an individual's success in life. This view has been reinforced by research exploring cultural differences in conceptions of intelligence.

Studies comparing the educational systems in Japan and Taiwan with those in the USA suggest that the Western stress on ability grouping minimises the importance of student, teacher and parental effort. The concept of differential ability sets a ceiling on what can be expected from a child. In Japan and Taiwan, pupils, with support from parents and teachers, are expected to put in additional effort if they are not successful (George 1989; Stevenson & Lee 1990). No one expects pupils to be removed from the classroom for special interventions or to make it easier to move ahead. There is no ability grouping in state schools prior to 10th grade in Japanese schools. The school day is longer and people are encouraged to work hard. Success is attributed to effort, failure to lack of effort. International comparisons of culture and pedagogy in primary schools have demonstrated that teachers in England and the USA identify more differences in ability between children than their counterparts in France, Russia and India where teachers attempt to progress classes together and place less importance on individual differences (Alexander 2000). The emphasis on ability in the UK acts to lower expectations of what pupils can achieve. Increased attainment at primary level in literacy and numeracy in recent years, where the majority of pupils have attained levels initially seen as 'average', supports this.

Recent conceptions of 'intelligence' have rejected the notion that it is a single entity, acknowledged its multifaceted nature and accepted that it develops in interaction with the environment. This has implications for ability grouping in schools. Grouping systems, e.g. streaming, that assume a single intelligence do not take account of variability in pupil performance across subjects. Acknowledging that ability depends on learning and is not fixed means that grouping systems must be sufficiently flexible to allow for the uneven development of academic skills. Children's motivation, effort and focus on academic work are not consistent in their intensity and change over time depending on circumstances. For this reason, progress is often erratic. Rigid grouping structures, where movement between groups is infrequent, lack the necessary flexibility. Groupings that take place within the class overcome these difficulties, enable teachers to monitor children's progress over time, adjusting groupings as necessary, and play down the importance of ability as opposed to effort.

The quality of teaching

Ability grouping structures, of themselves, do not raise attainment. Indeed, as we saw earlier, in mathematics, when the same teaching materials are used, mixed-ability teaching is more effective (Whitburn 2001). Recognition of the limitations of structured ability grouping as a means of raising standards has led to a focus on the quality of teaching. This, in part, depends on teachers' beliefs and expectations. What teachers 'think' influences 'what they do' (Clark & Peterson 1986; Carlgren *et al.* 1994). To raise attainment teachers need to have high expectations and aspirations for their pupils (Jussim *et al.* 1998). Ability grouping, of itself, influences teachers' expectations (Ireson & Hallam 2001). The capabilities of pupils in the lower groups tend to be underestimated, while those in the higher groups may be overestimated (Boaler 1997). Teachers perceive that they are matching the curriculum and teaching strategies to the needs of the learner. As we saw in Chapter 5 this leads to very different learning experiences for pupils, many of whom feel that work is set at an inappropriate level. To rectify this requires a change in teachers' thinking about ability, pupils' capabilities and the nature of teaching and learning.

Teachers' beliefs and their relationship to teaching and learning

If teachers' beliefs affect the way that they teach, what beliefs do 'effective' teachers hold? Effective teachers of literacy place a high priority on meaning and understanding, and focus on shared texts as a way of making connections between word, sentence and text explicit to pupils. They explain to pupils the importance of what is to be learned and make connections between different aspects of literacy, particularly reading and writing. They teach skills in a systematic and structured way and model, in a variety of ways, the processes involved in reading and writing. They conduct lessons briskly, and periodically refocus pupils' attention on the task in hand. They set time limits and provide clear time frames to maintain concentration. Lessons are concluded with a review of work completed. They hold strong coherent beliefs about teaching literacy which guide their selection of materials and approaches. They also have well developed systems for monitoring and assessment and use their findings in planning subsequent lessons (Medwell *et al.* 1998).

In numeracy, three contrasting teaching orientations: connectionist, transmission and discovery have been identified (Askew *et al.* 1997). The most effective teachers are those described as connectionist. They value getting pupils to think and talk about their learning and make connections between different aspects of maths and different perspectives regarding the same aspect. Highly effective teachers believe that the mathematical and pedagogical purposes underpinning classroom practices are as important as the practices themselves in determining effectiveness. They hold a coherent set of beliefs about learning mathematics, in particular, that being numerate involves using strategies that are both efficient and effective and rests on the development of a rich network of connections between different mathematical ideas. They believe that all children can become numerate and use teaching approaches which ensure that all pupils are challenged and stretched, not just the more able. They build upon pupils' existing strategies for calculating and help them to increase their efficiency. They encourage pupils to describe their methods and their reasoning and use these descriptions for developing understanding and establishing connections. Dialogue and shared imagery are used to enable the teacher to understand pupils' thinking and for pupils to access the teacher's knowledge. Discussion takes place with the whole class, in small groups and with individual pupils. Pupils are encouraged to use mental, written or electronic methods of calculation, whichever are the most effective for the current problem. Effective teachers adopt systematic assessment and recording methods to monitor pupils' progress and record pupil strategies for calculation which inform future planning. Those teachers described as less effective use assessment infrequently and as a means to check that what they have taught has been learned. It is not used to inform planning for future learning.

Effective teachers of literacy and numeracy have a deep understanding of their subject and have coherent beliefs about how it should be taught. They focus on meaning, making connections between various aspects of the subject, and ensuring that pupils see the relevance of what they are learning and are able to think about why they are doing what they are doing. All pupils are seen as capable of learning and are helped to build on what they can already do. Pupil progress is monitored carefully to enable the teacher to plan future activities and teaching. These teaching beliefs and activities are what underpin effective pupil learning and can be adopted in relation to a variety of pupil grouping contexts.

Classroom management

There have been many attempts to identify the characteristics of the effective teacher and what constitutes effective classroom practice (for reviews see Brophy & Good 1986; Creemers 1994; Tabberer 1994; Joyce *et al.* 1997; Wittrock 1986). Differences in classroom management, maintaining order, student activities, questioning skills, teaching methods and classroom climate have been explored. Teachers either display all of the effective behaviours or none (Creemers 1997).

There is considerable agreement regarding the generic skills that teachers require in relation to the management of the classroom (e.g. Brophy & Good 1986). They need to pay attention to the quantity and pace of instruction, giving information, questioning pupils, handling individual work and homework and also take account of the learning context. They need to have clear intentions and convey these to their pupils (Tabberer 1994; Bruner 1996). They routinise many operations in order to reduce the complexity of classroom activity. This enables them to focus their attention on dealing with those events that may disrupt learning. This constant monitoring has become known as 'withitness' (Kounin 1970). Teachers can adopt a range of strategies to manage the classroom but often prefer whole-class teaching because it reduces the level of complexity (Creemers & Tillema 1988). If this practice is adopted consistently the range of learning opportunities for pupils is considerably reduced. While training can prepare teachers for many aspects of classroom management, to develop high levels of expertise requires practice.

Much of the teacher's task centres on developing an appropriate classroom environment. Classrooms are complex settings with multiple dimensions operating simultaneously, immediately and unpredictably (Doyle 1986). The variety of possible interactions between teachers and pupils is enormous. Teachers need to learn how to manage this environment in a positive way (Brookover *et al.* 1979; Scheerens 1992). Neutral and warm environments have a strong relationship with achievement, while negative atmospheres can have a detrimental effect on pupils' progress (Soar & Soar 1979). The teacher has to ensure that pupils are maintained 'on task' in order to promote learning (Woods 1990). To achieve this, teachers have to be adept at making the work interesting and varied, giving attention to individuals, using humour and converting work to play. In addition, as pupils get older they wish to be treated with respect (Ruddock *et al.* 1996), with their rights and responsibilities acknowledged (Powell 1980).

While creating the appropriate environment for learning is important, this must not detract from a focus on academic work. Effective teachers tend to be business-like, task oriented, interacting primarily on a teacher–pupil basis, operating their classrooms as learning environments and spending most of their time on academic activities (Brophy & Good 1986). The least effective teachers tend to be too concerned with personal relationships and affective outcomes, or are disillusioned and bitter, dislike their students and concentrate on discipline and authority issues. Teachers whose pupils are the highest achievers assume personal responsibility for their teaching and the learning of their pupils, feel efficacious, have an internal locus of control, organise their classrooms, plan proactively on a daily basis, and display a 'can do' attitude (Tabberer 1994). Table 7.1 sets out a range of strategies that teachers can adopt to develop a classroom climate that engages and motivates learners.

Table 7.1 Classrooms that motivate pupils

Tasks
- Design activities that make learning interesting and that involve variety and personal challenge;
- Help learners establish realistic goals. With short-term goals, students view their class work as manageable, and they can focus on their progress and what they are learning;
- Help students develop organisational and management skills and effective task strategies.

Involvement and responsibility
- Give students opportunities to participate actively in the learning process – making choices, taking decisions;
- Help students develop the skills that will enable them to take responsibility for their learning.

Recognition
- Recognise individual student effort, attainment and improvement;
- Give all students opportunities to receive reward and recognition;
- Give recognition and rewards privately so that their value is not at the expense of others.

Grouping
- Provide opportunities for cooperative group work and peer interaction;
- Use a variety of grouping arrangements.

Evaluation
- Evaluate students for individual progress, improvement and mastery;
- Give students opportunities to improve their performance;
- Vary the methods of evaluation;
- Keep evaluations private.

Time
- Adjust task time requirements for students who have difficulty completing their work;
- Allow students opportunities to plan their work and progress at a rate optimal for them.

(Derived from the work of Ames 1992 and Epstein 1989)

Teacher–pupil relationships

The quality of the relationships between pupils and teachers is crucial for learning to be effective. One conceptualisation of the way that this relationship develops in practice is set out in Figure 7.1 (MacGilchrist *et al.* 1997). This model suggests that effective learning depends on a pact between the teacher and the learner where each brings aspects of themselves to the learning situation reflecting their different roles. For learning to be effective they contribute to the pact shared characteristics, needs, aims, aspirations and skills. These are interdependent and crucial for successful learning and development to take place.

A more detailed description of the way that teachers and learners negotiate in relation to specific tasks is set out in Figure 7.2 (Francis 1994). This model suggests that learners and teachers have 'different voices' with respect to learning and hear each other through a confusing filter. This is compounded by the classroom situation in which teachers have practical difficulty in dealing with individual pupils because of the size of classes. The model suggests that when work is undertaken on a task, teachers and learners can observe and evaluate progress and use this information to inform how future learning should be undertaken. If

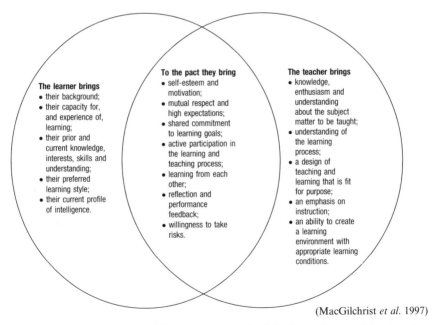

The learner brings
- their background;
- their capacity for, and experience of, learning;
- their prior and current knowledge, interests, skills and understanding;
- their preferred learning style;
- their current profile of intelligence.

To the pact they bring
- self-esteem and motivation;
- mutual respect and high expectations;
- shared commitment to learning goals;
- active participation in the learning and teaching process;
- learning from each other;
- reflection and performance feedback;
- willingness to take risks.

The teacher brings
- knowledge, enthusiasm and understanding about the subject matter to be taught;
- understanding of the learning process;
- a design of teaching and learning that is fit for purpose;
- an emphasis on instruction;
- an ability to create a learning environment with appropriate learning conditions.

(MacGilchrist *et al.* 1997)

Figure 7.1 The teaching and learning pact – the interdependence of the teacher and learner

there is more than one possible way of acting on the task the learner has to make a choice based on previous experience and the current situation. The teacher can provide guidance here. In this situation, the teacher and the individual learner need to demonstrate to each other their understandings of how a task should be done and why it should be done that way. Deficiencies in these 'learning conversations' can impede effective learning. In whole-class or large group discussions led by the teacher, these negotiations can be enacted in public as models for other pupils.

Pupil grouping for effective learning

The major factor in the effectiveness of groupings in raising attainment and maximising the positive aspects of personal and social development is that they offer sufficient flexibility to meet changing demands at school, class, group and individual levels. Highly structured systems, which involve regrouping across several classes and large numbers of pupils, tend to lack this flexibility. The most appropriate way for individual schools to develop flexibility in grouping depends on their size, resources and pupil intake. There is no simple 'off the shelf' recipe for success.

Pupil needs change over time and schools must be able to respond to them. However, implementation of new practices must take account of existing staff attitudes and allow time for discussion of different options so that staff have ownership of new systems. This requires that schools monitor the effectiveness of their grouping systems, not only in relation to academic attainment, but in relation to the personal and social educational outcomes of all their pupils. Efforts to make grouping practices more effective need to be regarded as an ongoing long-term commitment. There are no quick-fix solutions.

Evidence-based practice

The impetus for changing grouping systems has often been external to the school, e.g. government guidance, Ofsted inspections, the appointment of a new head teacher. If schools are to adopt flexible grouping to maximise the academic, personal and social development of their pupils they need to base their practice on evidence. This requires that schools develop ways of systematically monitoring:

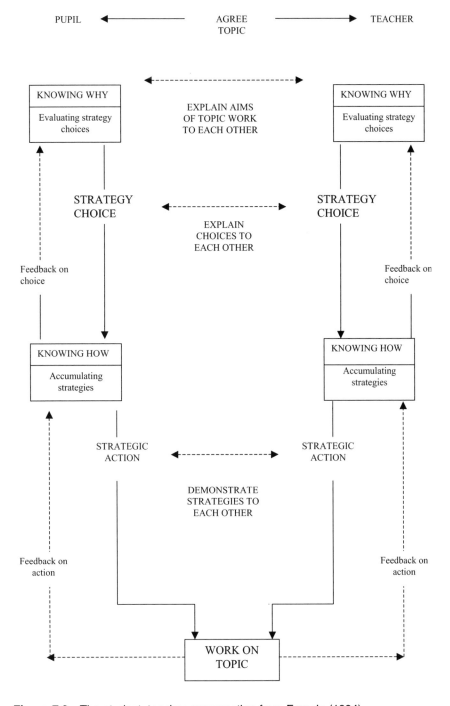

Figure 7.2 The student–teacher conversation from Francis (1994)

- progress across all curriculum subjects;
- pupils' attitudes towards learning and school;
- pupils' self-esteem; and
- levels of disaffection (through non-attendance, unauthorised absence and fixed-term and permanent exclusions).

These data can then be used to inform decisions about grouping structures between and within classes. Further information can be gained from providing pupils with opportunities to discuss their progress and experiences of grouping with their teachers.

If schools adopt such monitoring procedures and act upon the evidence that they provide there is the very real prospect of grouping structures evolving that are based on the learning needs of pupils rather than administrative convenience. Such learning-focused groupings could play a key role in raising educational attainment while enhancing pupils' personal and social development.

Chapter summary: overview and conclusions

Class structures in schools were designed for an industrial age.

The practice of rigidly structured ability grouping is underpinned by outdated conceptions of the nature of intelligence.

Modern conceptions of intelligence stress its multi-faceted nature and fluidity over time.

To take account of this groupings must be flexible.

Key to raising standards are:

- the quality of the teaching;
- high expectations of all pupils; and
- the relationships between staff and pupils within the school.

To optimise the positive effects of different types of grouping the school needs to monitor pupils' academic progress and personal and social development.

Groupings need to be established to meet the learning needs of pupils, not organisational convenience within the school.

Blandford, J.S. (1958) 'Standardised tests in junior schools with special reference to the effects of streaming on the constancy of results', *British journal of educational psychology* **28**, 170–3.

Blatchford, P. (1997) 'Pupils' self-assessments of academic attainment at 7, 11 and 16 years: effects of sex and ethnic group', *Educational psychology* **67**, 169–84.

Blenkin, G.M. & Kelly, A.V. (1987) *The primary curriculum: a process approach to curriculum planning*. London: Harper & Row.

Boaler, J. (1997) *Experiencing school mathematics: teaching styles, sex and setting*. Buckingham: Open University Press.

Board of Education (Great Britain) (1931) *The primary school*. London: HMSO.

Broadfoot, P. & Osborn, M. (1988) 'What professional responsibility means to teachers: national contexts and classroom contexts', *British journal of sociology of education* **9**(3), 265–87.

Brookover, W.B., Beady, C., Flood, P., Schweitzer, J. & Wisenbaker, J. (1979) *School social systems and student achievement: schools can make a difference*. New York: Praeger.

Brophy, J. & Good, T.L. (1986) 'Teacher behaviour and student achievement', in Wittrock, C.M. (ed.) *Handbook of research on teaching* (3rd edn). New York: MacMillan.

Bruner, J. (1996) *The culture of education*. Cambridge, Mass: Harvard University Press.

Burden, M., Emsley, M. & Constable, M. (1988) 'Encouraging progress in collaborative groupwork', *Education 3–13* **16**(1), 51–6.

Carlgren, I., Handal, G. & Vaage, S. (1994) *Teachers' minds and actions: research on teachers' thinking and practice*. London: Falmer Press.

Ceci, S.J. (1990) *On intelligence . . . more or less: a biological treatise on intellectual development*. Englewood Cliffs, New Jersey: Prentice Hall.

Chaplain, R. (1996) 'Pupils under pressure: coping with stress at school', in Rudduck, J., Chaplain, R. & Wallace, G. (eds) *School improvement: what can pupils tell us?* London: David Fulton Publishers.

Chapman, J.W. (1988) 'Learning disabled children's self-concepts', *Review of educational research*, **58**, 347–71.

Clark, C.M. & Peterson, P.L. (1986) 'Teachers' thought processes', in Brown, S. & McIntyre, D. (eds) (1993) *Making sense of teaching*. Buckingham: Open University Press.

Cohen, E.G. (1994) 'Restructuring the classroom: conditions for productive small groups', *Review of educational research* **64**, 1–35.

Creemers, B.P.M. (1994) *The effective classroom*. London: Cassell.

Creemers, B. (1997) *Effective schools and effective teachers: an international perspective*. Warwick: Centre for Research in Elementary and Primary School Education, University of Warwick.

Creemers, B. & Tillema, H. (1988) 'The Classroom as a Social/Emotional Environment', *Journal of classroom interaction* **23**(2), 1–7.

Croll, P. (1996) 'The National Curriculum and Special Educational Needs', in Croll, P. (ed.) *Teachers, pupils and primary schooling: continuity and change*. London: Cassell.

Croll, P. & Hastings, N.J. (1996) 'Teachers matter', in Croll, P. & Hastings, N. (eds) *Effective primary teaching: research-based classroom strategies*. London: David Fulton Publishers.

Croll, P. & Moses, D. (1985) *One in five: the assessment and incidence of Special Educational Needs*. London: Routledge & Kegan Paul.

Croll, P. & Moses, D. (1988) 'Teaching methods and time-on-task in junior classrooms', *Educational research* **30**(2), 90–7.

Crozier, S. & Kleinberg, S. (1987) 'Solving problems in a group', *Education 3–13* **15**(3), 37–41.

Daniels, J.C. (1961a) 'The effects of streaming in the primary schools: I what teachers believe', *British journal of educational psychology* **31**, 69–78.

Daniels, J.C. (1961b) 'The effects of streaming in the primary schools: II comparison of streamed and unstreamed schools', *British journal of educational psychology* **31**, 119–26.

Department for Education (1993) *Improving primary education – Patten* (DfE News 16/93). London: DfE.

Department for Education and Employment (1997) *Excellence in schools*. London: DfEE.

Department for Education and Employment (1998) *The National Literacy Strategy: framework for teaching*. London: DfEE.

Department for Education and Employment (1999) *The National Numeracy Strategy. Framework for teaching mathematics, from reception to year 6*. London: DfEE.

Department for Education and Employment/Qualifications and Curriculum Authority (1999) *The National Curriculum*. London: DfEE/QCA.

Department for Education and Employment (2000) *Organisation in the literacy hour and daily mathematics lesson*. www.dfee.gov.uk/circulars/dfeepub/jan00.

Department for Education and Employment (2001a) *Schools building on success*. London: DfEE.

Department for Education and Employment (2001b) *Schools achieving success*. London: DfEE.

Department for Education and Science (1978) *Primary education in England: a survey by HM Inspectors of Schools*. London: HMSO.

Department for Education and Science (1988) *Education Reform Act*. London: DfE.

Devine, D. (1993) 'A study of reading ability groups: primary school children's experiences and views', *Irish educational studies* **12**, 134–42.

Douglas, J.W.B. (1964) *The home and the school*. London: MacGibbon & Kee.

Doyle, W. (1986) 'Classroom organisation and management', in Wittrock, M.C. (ed.) *Handbook of research on teaching* (3rd edn). New York: MacMillan.

Dreeben, R. & Barr, R. (1988) 'Classroom composition and the design of instruction', *Sociology of education* **61**, 129–42.

Dunne, E. & Bennett, N. (1990) *Talking and learning in groups*. London: Macmillan.

Epstein, J. (1989) 'Family structures and student motivation: a developmental perspective', in Ames, C. & Ames, R. (eds) *Research on motivation and education, Vol 3*. New York: Academic Press.

Ferri, E. (1971) *Streaming two years later: a follow up of a group of pupils who attended streamed and nonstreamed junior schools.* London: NFER.

Francis, H. (1994) *Teachers listening to learners' voices: the thirteenth Vernon-Wall lecture.* Leicester: Education Section of the British Psychological Society.

Galton, M. (1981) 'Teaching groups in the junior school: a neglected art', *Schools organisation* **1**(2), 175–81.

Galton, M., Patrick, H., Appleyard, R., Hargreaves, L. & Bernbaum, G. (1987) *Curriculum provision in small schools: the PRISMS project, Final Report.* Leicester: University of Leicester.

Galton, M., Simon, B. & Croll, P. (1980) *Inside the primary classroom.* London: Routledge & Kegan Paul.

Galton, M. & Williamson, J. (1992) *Groupwork in the primary classroom.* London: Routledge.

Gardner, H. (1993) *Frames of mind: the theory of multiple intelligences.* New York: Basic Books.

Gardner, H. (1999) 'Are there additional intelligences? the case for naturalist, spiritual and existential intelligences', in Kane, J. (ed.) *Education, information and transformation.* Englewood Cliffs, NJ: Prentice Hall.

George, P. (1989) *The Japanese junior high school: a view from the inside.* Columbus, OH: National Middle School Association.

Gillborn, D. & Youdell, D. (2000) *Rationing education: policy, practice, reform and equity.* Buckingham: Open University Press.

Gipps, C., McCallum, B. & Hargreaves, E. (2000) *What makes a good primary school teacher?: expert classroom strategies.* London: Falmer.

Glaye, A. (1986) 'Outer appearances with inner experiences – towards a more holistic view of group-work', *Educational review* **38**(1), 45–56.

Gregory, R.P. (1984) 'Streaming, setting and mixed ability grouping in primary and secondary schools: some research findings', *Educational studies* **10**(3), 209–26.

Gregory, R.P. (1986) 'Mixed ability teaching – a rod for the teacher's back?', *Journal of applied educational studies* **15**(2), 56–61.

Gregory, R.P., Hackney, C. & Gregory, N.M. (1982) 'Corrective reading programme: an evaluation', *British journal of educational psychology* **52**, 33–50.

Gutierrez, R. & Slavin, R.E. (1992) 'Achievement effects of the non-graded elementary school: a best evidence synthesis', *Review of educational research* **62**, 333–76.

Hacker, R.G. & Rowe, M.J. (1993) 'A study of the effects of an organisation change from streamed to mixed-ability classes upon science classroom instruction', *Journal of research in science teaching* **30**(3), 223–31.

Hallam, S. (1996) *Improving school attendance.* Oxford: Heinemann.

Hallam, S. (1998) *Instrumental teaching: a practical guide to better teaching and learning.* Oxford: Heinemann.

Hallam, S. (2002) *Ability grouping in schools: a literature review.* London: Institute of Education, University of London.

Hallam, S. & Ireson, J. (1999) 'Pedagogy in the secondary school', in Mortimore, P. (ed.) *Understanding pedagogy and its impact on learning.* London: Sage Publications.

Hallam, S., Ireson, J., Chaudhury, I., Lister, V., Davies, J. & Mortimore, P. (1999a) *Ability grouping practices in the primary school: a survey of what schools are doing.* Paper presented at British Educational Research Association (BERA) conference, University of Sussex, Brighton, 2–5 September.

Hallam, S., Ireson, J., Davies, J. & Mortimore, P. (1999b) *School ethos and primary pupils' perceptions of ability grouping.* Paper presented at the conference of BERA, University of Sussex, Brighton, 2–5 September 1999.

Hallam, S. & Toutounji, I. (1996a) *What do we know about the grouping of pupils by ability?* London: Institute of Education, University of London.

Hallam, S. & Toutounji, I. (1996b) 'What do we know about grouping pupils by ability?', *Education review* **10**(2), 62–70.

Harlen, W. & Malcolm, H. (1997) *Setting and streaming: a research review* (Using Research Series 18). Edinburgh: SCRE.

Harwood, D. (1989) 'The nature of teacher–pupil interaction in the active tutorial work approach: using interaction analysis to evaluate student-centred approaches', *British educational research journal* **15**, 177–94.

Hastings, N.J., Schwieso, J. & Wheldall, K. (1996) 'A place for learning', in Croll, P. & Hastings, N. (eds) *Effective primary teaching.* London: David Fulton Publishers.

Hastings, N.J. & Schwieso, J. (1995) 'Tasks and tables: the effects of seating arrangements on task engagement in primary schools', *Educational research* **37**(3), 279–91.

HMI, Department of Education and Science (1978) *Mixed ability work in comprehensive schools.* London: HMSO.

HMI, Department of Education and Science (1979) *Aspects of secondary education in England.* London: HMSO.

Howe, M.J.A. (1997) *IQ in question: the truth about intelligence.* London: Sage.

Hughes, M. (1993) *Flexible learning: evidence examined.* Stafford: Network Educational Press Ltd.

Ireson, J. (1996) 'Pupil grouping and reading activities in the teaching of reading', paper presented at the British Educational Research Association conference, Lancaster.

Ireson, J. & Hallam, S. (1999) 'Raising standards: is ability grouping the answer?', *Oxford review of education* **25**(3), 343–58.

Ireson, J. & Hallam, S. (2000) 'Raising standards: is ability grouping the answer?', in Collins, J. & Cook, D. (eds) *Understanding learning: influences and outcomes.* London: Sage Publications.

Ireson, J. & Hallam, S. (2001) *Ability grouping in education.* London: Sage.

Jackson, B. (1964) *Streaming: an education system in miniature.* London: Routledge & Kegan Paul.

Jaques, D. (2000) *Learning in groups.* London: Kogan Page.

Johnson, D.W. & Johnson, R.T. (1975) *Learning together and alone.* Englewood Cliffs, NJ: Prentice Hall.

Joyce, B., Calhoun, E. & Hopkins, D. (1997) *Models of learning – tools for teaching.* Buckingham: Open University Press.

Jussim, L., Smith, A., Madon, S. & Palumbo, P. (1998) 'Teacher expectations', in Brophy, J. (ed.) *Advances in Research on Teaching*, vol. 7. Greenwich, CT: JAI Press.

Kerry, T. & Sands, M.K. (1984) 'Classroom organisation and learning', in Wragg, E.C. (ed.) *Classroom teaching skills: the research findings of the teacher education project.* London: Routledge.

Kounin, J. (1970) *Discipline and group management in classrooms.* New York: Holt, Rinehart & Winston.

Kulik, C.-L.C. & Kulik, J.A. (1982) 'Effects of ability grouping on secondary school students: a meta-analysis of evaluation findings', *American educational research journal* **19**, 415–28.

Kulik, J. A. (1991) 'An analysis of the research on ability grouping: historical and contemporary perspectives', Storrs: University of Connecticut, National Research Center on the Gifted and Talented (ERIC Document Reproduction Service No. ED 350 777).

Kulik, J.A. & Kulik, C.-L.C. (1987) 'Effects of ability grouping on student achievement', *Equity and excellence* **23**(1–2), 22–30.

Kulik, J.A. & Kulik, C.-L.C. (1992) 'Meta-analytic findings on grouping programs', *Gifted child quarterly* **36**(2), 73–7.

Kutnick, P. (1994) 'Use and effectiveness of groups in classrooms: towards a pedagogy', in Kutnick, P. & Rogers, C. (eds) (1994) *Groups in schools.* London: Cassell.

Kutnick, P. & Rogers, C. (eds) (1994) *Groups in schools.* London: Cassell.

Kyriacou, C. (1997) *Effective teaching in schools: theory and practice.* Cheltenham: Stanley Thornes.

Lee, J. & Croll, P. (1995) 'Streaming and subject specialism at key stage 2: a survey in two local authorities', *Educational Studies* **21**(2), 155–65.

Lou, Y., Abrami, P.C., Spence, J.C., Poulsen, C., Chambers, B. & d'Apollonia, S. (1996) 'Within-class grouping: a meta-analysis', *Review of educational research* **66**(4), 423–58.

MacGilchrist, B., Myers, K. & Reed, J. (1997) *The intelligent school.* London: Paul Chapman Publishing.

MacIntyre, H. & Ireson, J. (2002) 'Within-class ability grouping: placement of pupils in groups and self-concept', *British educational research journal* **28**(2), 249–64.

Marsh, H.W. (1990) *Self Description Questionnaire II Manual.* Sydney: University of Western Sydney.

Medwell, J., Wray, D., Poulson, L. & Fox, R. (1998) *Effective teachers of literacy.* Exeter: University of Exeter.

Metz, M.H. (1978) *Classrooms and corridors: the crisis of authority in desegregated secondary schools.* Berkeley: University of California Press.

Miller, B.A. (1990) 'A review of the quantitative research on multi-grade instruction', *Research in rural education* **7**(1), 1–8.

Mortimore, P. (1992) 'Issues in school effectiveness', in Reynolds, D. & Cuttance, P. (eds) *School effectiveness: research, policy and practice*. London: Cassell.

Mortimore, P., Sammons, P., Ecob, R., Stoll, L. & Lewis, D. (1988) *School matters: the junior years*. Salisbury: Open Books.

Nasati, B. & Clements, D. (1991) 'Research on co-operative learning: implications for practice', *School psychology review* **20**, 110–31.

Oakes, J. (1985) *Keeping track: how schools structure inequality*. New Haven: Yale University Press.

Ofsted (1997) *Standards and quality in education 1995–1996: the annual report of Her Majesty's Chief Inspector of Schools*. London: Office for Standards in Education.

Ofsted (1998a) *Standards and quality in education 1996–1997: the annual report of Her Majesty's Chief Inspector of Schools*. London: Office for Standards in Education.

Ofsted (1998b) *Setting in primary schools: a report from the office of Her Majesty's Chief Inspector of Schools*. London: Office for Standards in Education.

Ofsted (2000) *The National Numeracy Strategy: the first year*. London: Office for Standards in Education.

Ofsted (2001) *Standards and quality in education 1999–2000: the annual report of Her Majesty's Chief Inspector of Schools*. London: Office for Standards in Education.

Pallas, A.M., Entwisle, D.R., Alexander, K.L. & Stluka, M.F. (1994) 'Ability-group effects: instructional, social, or institutional?', *Sociology of education* **67**(1), 27–46.

Peverett, R. (1994) 'Teaching 9–11 year olds', in National Commission of Education *Insights into education and training*. Oxford: Heinemann.

Plowden Report (1967) *Children and their primary schools: report of the Central Advisory Council for Education in England*. London: HMSO.

Pollard, A., Broadfoot, P., Croll, P., Osborn, M. & Abbott, D. (1994) *Changing English primary schools?* London: Cassell.

Powell, M. (1980) 'The beginning teacher evaluation study: a brief history of a major research project', in Denham, C. and Lieberman, A. (eds) *Time to learn*. Washington, DC: National Institute of Education.

Pratt, D. (1986) 'On the merits of multi-age classrooms', *Research in rural education* **3**(3), 111–15.

Reid, M.E., Clunies-Ross, L.R., Goacher, B. & Vile, D. (1982) *Mixed ability teaching: problems and possibilities*. Windsor: NFER-Nelson.

Reuman, D.A. (1989) 'How social comparison mediates the relation between ability-grouping practices and students' achievement expectancies in mathematics', *Journal of educational psychology* **81**, 178–89.

Richardson, K. (1991) 'Reasoning with Raven – in and out of context', *British journal of educational psychology* **61**(2), 129–38.

Richardson, K. (1999) *The making of intelligence*. London: Weidenfeld and Nicolson.

Roeders, P. (1989) 'The coaching classroom: increasing school effectiveness by a child oriented, creatively based educational method', Paper given to 12th

International School Psychology Association (ISPA) Conference, Ljublyana, August.

Rudd, W.G.A. (1956) 'The psychological effects of streaming by attainment with special reference to a group of selected children', *British journal of educational psychology* **28**, 47–60.

Rudduck, J., Chaplain, R. & Wallace, G. (1996) *School improvement: what can pupils tell us?* London: David Fulton Publishers.

Sammons, P., Hillman, J. & Mortimore, P. (1995) *Key characteristics of effective schools: a review of school effectiveness research.* London: Office for Standards in Education.

Sands, M.K. & Kerry, T. (eds) (1982) *Mixed ability teaching.* London: Croom Helm.

Scheerens, J. (1992) *Effective schooling: research, theory and practice.* London: Cassell.

Scottish Education Department Inspectors of Schools (1992) *Using ethos indicators in primary school self-evaluation: taking account of the views of pupils, parents and teachers.* Edinburgh: Scottish Office Education Department.

Scottish Office (1996) *Achievement for all: a report on selection within schools.* Edinburgh: HMSO.

Sharp, C., Osgood, J. & Flanagan, N. (1999) *The benefits of study support: a review of opinion and research.* London: DfEE.

Slavin, R. (1983) *Co-operative learning.* New York: Longman.

Slavin, R.E. (1987) 'Ability grouping and student achievement in elementary schools: a best evidence synthesis', *Review of educational research* **57**(3), 293–336.

Slavin, R.E. (1990) 'Co-operative learning', in Rogers, C. & Kutnick, P., *The social psychology of the primary school.* London: Routledge.

Slavin, R.E. & Karweit, N.L. (1985) 'Effects of whole class, ability grouped and individualised instruction on mathematics achievement', *American educational research journal* **22**(3), 351–67.

Snyder, B.R. (1971) *The hidden curriculum.* New York: Knopf.

Soar, R.S. & Soar, R.M. (1979) 'Emotional climate and management', in Peterson, P. & Walberg, H. (eds) *Research on teaching: concepts, findings and implications.* Berkeley, CA: McCutchan.

Sternberg, R.J. (1984) 'Toward a triarchic theory of human intelligence', *Behavioural and brain sciences* **7**, 269–315.

Stevenson, H. & Lee, S. (1990) 'Contexts of achievement: a study of American, Chinese and Japanese children', *Monographs of the society for research in child development* **221**(55), No. 1–2. Chicago: University of Chicago.

Sukhnandan, L. & Lee, B. (1998) *Streaming, setting and grouping by ability: a review of the literature.* Slough: NFER.

Swing, S. & Peterson, P. (1982) 'The relationships of student ability and small-group interaction to student achievement', *American educational research journal* **19**, 259–74.

Tabberer, R. (1994) *School and teacher effectiveness.* Slough: NFER.

Tann, S. (1981) 'Grouping and groupwork', in Simon, B. & Willcocks, J. (eds) *Research and practice in the primary classroom*. London: Routledge & Kegan Paul.

Tough, P. (1977) *The development of meaning: a study of use of language*. London: Allen & Unwin.

Troman, G. (1988) 'Getting it right: selection and setting in a 9–13 years middle school', *British journal of sociology of education* **9**(4), 403–22.

Troyna, B. (1992) 'Ethnicity and the organisation of learning groups: a case study', *Educational research* **34**(1), 45–55.

Turney, A.H. (1931) 'The status of ability grouping', *Educational administration and supervision* **17**, 21–42, 110–27.

Vanfossen, B.E., Jones, J.D. & Spade, J.Z. (1987) 'Curriculum tracking and status maintenance', *Sociology of education* **60**, April, 104–22.

Veenman, S. (1995) 'Cognitive and noncognitive effects of multigrade and multi-age classes: a best evidence synthesis', *Review of educational research* **65**(4), 319–81.

Waxman, H.C., Wang, M.C., Anderson, K.A. & Walberg, H.J. (1985) 'Synthesis of research on the effects of adaptive education', *Educational leadership* **43**(1), 27–9.

Webb, N. (1983) 'Predicting learning from student interaction: defining the interaction variable', *Educational psychologist* **18**, 33–41.

Webb, N. (1985) 'Verbal interaction and learning in peer directed groups', *Theory into practice* **24**(1), 32–9.

Webb, N. (1989) 'Peer interaction and learning in small groups', *International journal of educational research* **13**, 21–39.

Webb, N. (1991) 'Task-related verbal interaction and mathematics learning in small groups', *Journal of research in mathematics education* **22**, 366–89.

Wheldall, K., Morris, M., Vaughan, P. & Ng, Y.Y. (1981) 'Rows versus tables: an example of behavioural ecology in two classes of eleven-year-old children', *Educational psychology* **1**(2), 27–44.

Wheldall, K. & Olds, D. (1987) 'Of sex and seating: the effects of mixed and same-sex seating arrangements in junior classrooms', *New Zealand journal of educational studies* **22**(1), 71–85.

Whitburn, J. (2001) 'Effective classroom organisation in primary schools: mathematics', *Oxford review of education* **27**(3), 411–28.

Willig, C.J. (1963) 'Social implication of streaming in junior schools', *Educational research* **5**, 151–4.

Wittrock, M. (ed.) (1986) *Handbook of research on teaching* (3rd edn). New York: MacMillan.

Woods, P. (1990) *The happiest days? how pupils cope with school*. London: Falmer Press.

Wragg, E.C. (ed.) (1984) *Classroom teaching skills: the research findings of the teacher education project*. London: Routledge.

Index